we

we

reviving social hope

Ronald Aronson

The University of Chicago Press • *Chicago & London*

The University of Chicago Press, Chicago 60637
The University of Chicago Press, Ltd., London
© 2017 by The University of Chicago

Published 2017. Printed in the United States of America

26 25 24 23 22 21 20 19 18 17   1 2 3 4 5

ISBN-13: 978-0-226-33466-0 (cloth)
ISBN-13: 978-0-226-33483-7 (e-book)
DOI: 10.7208/chicago/9780226334837.001.0001

Library of Congress Cataloging-in-Publication Data

Names: Aronson, Ronald, 1938– author.
Title: We : reviving social hope / Ronald Aronson.
Description: Chicago ; London : The University of Chicago Press, 2017. |
Includes bibliographical references and index.
Identifiers: LCCN 2016052006 | ISBN 9780226334660 (cloth : alk. paper) |
ISBN 9780226334837 (e-book)
Subjects: LCSH: Hope—Social aspects. | Social participation. | Progress.
Classification: LCC BD216 .A765 2017 | DDC 302/.14—dc23 LC record
available at https://lccn.loc.gov/2016052006

♾ This paper meets the requirements of ANSI/NISO Z39.48-1992
(Permanence of Paper).

For Phyllis

Contents

Acknowledgments

This book has developed over a lifetime of writing, reflection, teaching, and political action. I have tried to make clear my many intellectual debts throughout the text, but two people deserve special homage. The first is my mentor, Herbert Marcuse, with whom I studied the history of ideas at Brandeis University. The second is Jean-Paul Sartre, whose ideas I have interacted with for fifty years. This book's questions, ideas, and arguments slowly took shape in *Jean-Paul Sartre: Philosophy in the World* (1980), *The Dialectics of Disaster: A Preface to Hope* (1983), *"Stay Out of Politics": A Philosopher Views South Africa* (1990), *After Marxism* (1995), and *Living without God* (2008). It received its current formulation in the 2012 Richard Burke Lecture at Oakland University. Some of its themes were developed in my farewell lecture at Wayne State University, "Whatever Happened to Progress?"; at that university's Humanities Center; before the United Kingdom Society for Sartrean Studies; at meetings of the Sartre Society of North America; and at the Diverse Lineages of Existentialism conference in St. Louis. Themes and portions of this book have appeared in *History and Theory, The Nation, New Politics, Social Research, Sartre Studies International,* and the *Boston Review.* Much of the manuscript was pondered and corrected at the Café Muse in Royal Oak, Michigan, where I owe special thanks to chef Greg Reyner and his staff.

Friends and colleagues who have discussed the project, read portions of it, and/or have made specific suggestions include Pamela Aronson, Hannah Aronson-Paxton, Bob Deneweth, Matt Eshleman, Ian Fletcher, Steve Fraser, Henry Giroux, Alice Golin, Steve Golin, Jennifer Hart, Chris Johnson, Ira Konigsberg, Charles Rooney, Anthony Rudolf, Paul Schaurt, Fran Shor, and Barbara Weill. The entire manuscript was read by Richard Bachmann, Beck Pitt, David Sprintzen, and Ernie Benjamin, and their comments have helped shape its final form. Simon Waxman edited the manuscript and provided invaluable intellectual and stylistic guidance. Phyllis Aronson and David Brent have been essential to the project from its beginning many years ago until now—encouraging me, demanding that I be clear, helping me find my voice, and gently reminding me to not shout.

A Note on We

Evgeny Zamyatin's novel *We* was begun in 1919, completed in 1921, and first published in 1924 in the United States. Denied publication in the Soviet Union until 1988, it describes a totalitarian society several hundred years in the future. Its members, called Numbers, are regimented and treated as cogs in a vast machine and regulated in precise detail by the Tables, a kind of *Official Railroad Guide* to every aspect of life in the United State that governs the whole earth.

> The Tables transformed each one of us, actually, into a six-wheeled steel hero of a great poem. Every morning, with six-wheeled precision, at the same hour, at the same minute, we wake up, millions of us at once. At the very same hour, millions like one, we begin our work, and millions like one, we finish it. United into a single body with a million hands, at the very same second, designated by the Tables, we carry the spoons to our mouths; at the same second we all go out to walk, go to the auditorium, to the halls for the Taylor exercises, and then to bed.[1]

The Numbers even have prescribed "personal hours" and personal relationships, which are also strictly regulated.

> We were down in the street. The avenue was crowded. On days when the weather is so beautiful, the afternoon personal hour is usually the hour of the supplementary walk. As always, the big Musical Tower was playing the March of the United State with all its pipes. The Numbers, hundreds, thousands of Numbers in light blue unifs (probably a derivative of the ancient uniform) with golden badges on the chest—the State number of each one, male or female—the Numbers were walking slowly, four abreast, exaltedly keeping step. I, we four, were but one of the innumerable waves of a powerful torrent: to my left, 0-90 (if one of my long-haired ancestors were writing this a thousand years ago he would probably call her by that funny word, mine); to my right, two unknown Numbers, a she-Number and a he-Number.[2]

In this dystopian novel the *we* is imposed on the individuals, or in a sense it takes their place as each of them suppresses his or her own *I*. Individual choice, to the extent that it still exists, is to fit in and lose almost all sense of oneself as a unique being, or to assert this, to rebel, and to face disaster. Thus the *we* does not form as individuals collectively agree: their unanimity is not of their own doing. However the United State came into being, its goal is to impose happiness by eliminating freedom and difference. The leaders have created a policing apparatus on the lookout for the slightest deviation that might undermine the sense of unanimity. All of which is to say that Zamyatin's title is meant ironically.

The novel reflects a twentieth-century world in which individuals were under assault by the society. Zamyatin's *We* is one of the chronicles of that assault, followed by, among others, Aldous Huxley's *Brave New World*, George Orwell's *1984*, and, in very different registers, Allen Ginsberg's *Howl* and then Herbert Marcuse's *One-Dimensional Man*.

In this twenty-first century the situation has become rather different. The last century's totalitarian societies have been destroyed or overthrown, leaving behind an indelible memory of their oppressiveness as well as their hideous parodies in North Korea and Islamic State. But in a sense it is now society and its most vital purposes that are under assault by its individuals— "in a sense" because the whole, society and individuals, results from a number of deranged social processes to be described in this book. From the climate crisis to neoliberal globalization, from the "precariat" to the imperatives of the consumer society, today's *I* is a distorted individualism that is no less a lie than was the twentieth century's *we*. Instead, the *we* that emerges in opposition to today's trends is not Zamyatin's oppressive and false collectivity that destroys social hope, but any of the active, democratic collectivities that revive this hope again and again. If the twentieth-century problem was *we*, perhaps then a very different *we* may point toward a solution for our time. If so, history will have indeed redefined the meaning of *we*.

Chapter 1
Hope in Trouble

Today the hope that matters most has fallen on hard times. Even after the catastrophes of the twentieth century the great modern hope had persisted "that things will one day finally get better," in Theodore Adorno's words—"that one day human beings will be allowed to breathe easily."[1] But today we are losing the hope of a better society and a better world, and even the collective consciousness that can pose such goals. Who still anticipates the continued spread of political and social equality and democracy? Who still banks on the collective force of workers and other ordinary people? Who still thinks that our children's and grandchildren's lives can be made better than our own? Who still expects that the development of science and technology and the spread of education will make the world more humane and livable? And who still sees themselves as belonging to a collectivity capable of making any of these things happen?

The belief in Progress was one version of the modern faith. Remarkably, it withstood the catastrophes of the first part of the twentieth century to reach its peak during the thirty glorious years of 1945–75. Only then did it begin to be rejected as an obsolete "grand narrative," and by now, intellectually speaking at least, we live "after Progress." Indeed, a "loathing of modernity" has become so widespread among intellectuals today that even proofs of a massive historical reduction of violence cannot succeed in counteracting it.[2]

To live after Progress is to share a civilizational mood of disillusionment and discouragement, in part because one of the main engines of Progress has turned out to have such negative consequences. Contemporary capitalism brings everything we do, touch, and are, increasingly under the imperative for profit, causing incessant change with little regard for human and environmental consequences. All corners of existence are subjected increasingly to a kind of free-market totalitarianism, a maelstrom of "growth" and "development" that sweeps everything in its path.

All our education and free elections, our medical science and economic productivity, our instant communications and psychological self-knowledge, do not make our world more hospitable, democratic, fairer, and more just. Nor do they give us heart that the forces shaping our lives are being brought under our collective control. The opposite is happening: as the impersonal force of "the market" rules more and more areas of life, as people see themselves increasingly as separated, isolated individuals, the damage to the environment becomes impossible to ignore. Both in the United States and Europe, existing political arrangements seem increasingly impotent to deal with the problems issuing from the "economization" of all areas of life.

Our world of shrunken hope generates an abundance of lesser hopes. We recycle our garbage. We donate to environmental causes. We may even demonstrate against the endless war. We work to save the whales and the wolves, we donate to Planned Parenthood, and we sign petitions, but we know that these never add up to something larger.

People live fervently by narrowed and individual hopes, sharing them among family and friends, finding them reflected in churches and in the media. We work out and eat carefully. We closely follow the latest advice about prostate and breast screening. We say "I love you" to each other and our children a dozen times a day. We dream of moving to someplace where living conditions are better. We read books and search websites that promise help in finding our bearings amidst the maelstrom.

But what has become of the great political and historical goal of making our collective life better, of doing away with oppression, of creating conditions in which all humans can finally breathe easily? What has become of the common good? And what has happened to those who once dreamed of, and acted upon, that different kind of progress—yes, the growth of individual empowerment as today, but intertwined with democratic control, social equality, and what Herbert Marcuse called "the pacification of existence"?

This has been the project of the left, those tens and hundreds of millions who, beginning with the revolutions that inaugurated the modern world, sympathized with, actively created, joined, and participated in the vast variety of social movements trying to bring about what is now disingenuously called "progressive" change. I am speaking of those who in large ways and small have created the various modern visions of social justice. They have fought for a living wage, equality, and democracy— through thinking, talking, and writing, and through marches, demonstrations, sit-ins, occupations, strikes, and revolutions. The left: philosophes, republicans, sans-culottes, Chartists, anarchists, socialists, communists, trade unionists, abolitionists, suffragists, Freedom Riders, civil rights activists, anticolonial and liberation movements, antiwar and antinuclear activists, feminists, native and Hispanic movements, and gay and lesbian activists—the climate of change they created, their sympathizers, their ideas and arguments, their victories and defeats, their organizations, and their sheer energy and courage have been decisive in shaping the world as we know it.

Of course, on the negative side, so have fascist movements, the forces of segregation and apartheid as well as colonialism and religious fundamentalism, and organizations and systems built around the defense of privilege and inequality. Those on the right also have their hopes, and they struggle fiercely to assert them. But they do not believe, nor does their functioning reflect, that all people have equal worth. Nor, when they act collectively for a common cause, do they demonstrate a sense of wider human solidarity. Outside the left, moreover, democratic functioning is not generally expected as a norm of collective action. Even when movements of the right show compassion, it does not stem from the root conviction that everyone belongs equally to the same human family but is rather an impulse of charity, which often keeps the less fortunate in a lower status. People on the right do not come together to abolish special privileges, but to assert them. To be sure, from workers' to women's to LGBT movements, currents of the left have indeed voiced demands of specific groups, but have done so out of a deep commitment to universal equality.

Outside the left there have indeed been other kinds of social hopes, narrower and exclusionary hopes, antidemocratic ones. But when anyone asks the broad questions about social hope today, such as "Is there reason to hope?" or "Is there hope for humanity?" they have in mind human beings as such, the entire human family, all of us together. To speak this way implies our common well-being as it has come to be defined historically—by the left. Its key values did not drop from the sky; democracy and equality, solidarity and freedom, and the ability to "breathe easily" have deep roots. They are civilization's key values. Without even knowing it, in asking about hope generally we are speaking from the left.

Yes, a lynch mob operates out of a kind of social hope. But it is fair to call it a twisted hope, not unlike that of the Donald Trump movement or the United Kingdom Independence Party. Their racism expresses an antisocial social hope. Compared with the hopes of the left, there is a despair in this hope that excludes.

Looking back on the recent history of the left's hopes is a bit like reading the story of the Joad family in John Steinbeck's *The Grapes of Wrath*. Loss follows upon loss, defeat builds upon defeat. Just when things cannot seem to get any worse, they do. The family is forced to shift ground and regroup continually, but they adapt each time as the space available for survival diminishes with each new blow from police, vigilantes, growers, and nature. Almost everything is lost, but the survivors keep on.

What makes Steinbeck's book hopeful at the end is Ma's

determination to keep the family together, Tom's decision to follow Casey's direction and join the wider struggle, and the instinctive solidarity Rose of Sharon shows when she nurses the starving man. Steinbeck wanted his readers to see an entire people transforming its sense of individual and personal suffering into a shared militancy: those caught up in such social evils would one day cohere into an unstoppable transformative force. But the day never came. And, like Steinbeck himself, those who most wholeheartedly embraced this vision and the Enlightenment's hopes have become disillusioned. In contrast, more than one hundred years ago a Yiddish political-literary journal was founded by Jewish socialists, one which continues to be published, having long outlived its expectant world. It is called *Di Tsukunft: The Future.* Who can imagine launching a political-literary journal with such a name today, in any language?

Some readers will lose no time in pointing out the universalizing assumptions behind these first pages, the "grand narrative" they embody, their sense of loss. Perhaps this disposition to speak about "we" is *the* problem after all? Yet I write in an unrepentant mood, as a political and philosophical partisan of *the* modern left project. When this project's world seemed to be passing, in 1979, Jean-François Lyotard described the "postmodern condition" in which the left vision was becoming obsolete. The New Left was fragmenting, or perhaps becoming differentiated, into the "identity politics" of multiple movements and perspectives. The different "faces of oppression" included, in Iris Young's formulation, marginalization, powerlessness, exploitation, cultural imperialism, and violence.[3]

From these experiences it had become difficult to think of a single left anymore, and this meant abandoning any coherent analysis or universal vision, along with their hope for creating a better world.

Since the 1970s, of course, the new social movements have kept many specific struggles going and at times have won spectacular results, such as the massive recent cultural turnabout concerning gays and lesbians. But if I still describe such movements as belonging to "the left," it is no less true that they have developed in ways such that their subjects no longer see themselves as part of a larger force and its broad cause of social justice. They now identify as discrete groups suffering specific oppressions, and demand their human rights as groups and individuals.

It is a puzzling picture for those of us who think in terms of "the left" and its onetime hopes. Collectively we have lost our bearings, but thousands of groups are in motion, batons are being passed between generations, transformative energy is everywhere. Every outrage against people and nature seems to be countered by a mobilization, a movement, a protest, an organization. Sometimes these briefly rekindle an overarching spirit: the Great Recession gave rise first to the Indignatos in Spain, and then spectacularly to Occupy everywhere. But despite the hope it momentarily kindled. Occupy vanished with few traces, seemingly leaving nothing behind but talk of "the 99 percent" and "the 1 percent" in a world of increasing inequality.

The modern left and its project are often seen as only a fleeting hope or, worse, an illusion.[4] From the point of view of identity politics, its vision can be dismissed as a Eurocentric metanarrative of straight white male workers and intellectuals, its "we" an "embarrassing macro-binary from the days of unity and solidarity."[5] It is accused of unreflectively subordinating women, racial and ethnic minorities, and gays and lesbians, and a single unified movement is regarded as unthinkable now that these others have become active on their own behalf.[6] If so, the demise of the left and its universalizing project will be best captured not by my above narrative of loss, but by asserting that subordinated individuals and groups have indeed *found* their bearings, which are fated to be specific and diverse from now on, along with their particular hopes.

But a sense of "the Movement," a comprehensive left vision, is more than nostalgia, because its possibility is deeply rooted in two realities. One of these is our common human identity, the other our common global situation. First, with all its complexities and contradictions, and however differentially, we all belong to an evolving world climate of social morality. In and through all particularities and contestations, humans today share a general sensibility—violated here, institutionalized there, appealed to elsewhere—built up over the course of human history. There is indeed a history of freedom, and in this sense certain specific movements—for example, toward gay marriage—are inconceivable without others, such as the New Left.[7] Second, our common situation is decisively shaped by global capitalism. The savage inequalities it has imposed over the past generation have been provoking new mass movements in several countries. Controlling its other immediate and destructive consequence, climate change, is provoking a collective struggle to protect our common home, one based on a universal vision and a common hope. Lyotard once wrote that "the very notion of reaching unanimity has been abandoned."[8] But after the Great Recession and in the face of climate change, his postmodern reconsideration demands to be reconsidered.

A no less basic challenge to the Enlightenment project and its leftist hopes has been mounted over the same period of time by neoliberalism. As discussed by Wendy Brown, its effects reach far beyond the capitalist offensive that has been reducing the welfare state, privatizing state functions and assets, shrinking the presence of labor unions, deregulating and financializing economic life, and bringing political life under the increasing influence of corporations and the very wealthy. Neoliberalism, "a peculiar form of reason that configures all aspects of existence in economic terms, is quietly undoing basic elements of democracy." The top-to-bottom marketization of all aspects of daily life "is converting the distinctly political character, meaning, and operation of democracy's constituent elements into *economic ones*"[9] as market logic and metrics have infiltrated government, education, culture, and the law. Indeed, individuals are more and more being treated and learning to treat themselves entrepreneurially, as bundles of "human capital."[10]

Brown's analysis adds to discussions among sociologists like Ulrich Beck, Zygmunt Baumann, and Anthony Giddens about the "individualized society" in which individuals have been made to be responsible for themselves as never before. Jürgen Habermas once described the lifeworld as becoming "colonized" by the economic system, and by now precious little free space remains. As Michel Foucault explored in the 1978–79 Collège de France lectures, civilization itself seems to be taking a new turn.[11] Brown speaks of his *Birth of Biopolitics* as an "appreciation of neoliberalism as a form of political reason and governing that reaches from the state to the soul, and not simply as economic policy."[12]

If this is so, and given the other changes mentioned so far in this chapter, aren't I dawdling by talking about hope? Isn't it politics rather than this rather odd species of philosophy that is needed today? From an activist perspective, a time-honored reflex would seem to demand assessing the terrain of battle and the balance of forces; how to restore the flagging sense of a community, the waning sense of collective participation in creating a collective future? How to overcome the usurpa- tion of *Homo politicus* by *Homo oeconomicus?* How to move toward more equal, more democratic social policies and an environmentally sustainable economy? Or, if we admit that there is a crisis of social vision and action, what then seems demanded is a focused and concrete rethinking of goals, both broad and specific. This might include, for example, asking who will be the subject of the future movement, how to attack the ascendant social logic, how much reform can be achieved within existing economic, social, and political structures, where the structures themselves need rethinking, and what sorts of transformations are necessary and possible today. What are the prospects for initiating significant social change and ecological protection within existing political channels; and beyond these, are alternative strategies possible?

These are important questions, demanding study and ex- periment in a number of different directions. But too quickly depicting the crisis of hope as a call to arms risks avoiding confronting what can only be called our civilizational malady. To try to revive movements when we are no longer animated by their guiding assumptions is to arrest the usual suspects. To comprehend our situation, it is necessary to understand what exactly is the hope that is being eroded. What kind of entity is social hope, and what does it mean to say that we have been losing it?

The hope I am concerned with is not merely an attitude, or a mood, or a feeling—all of which emphasize its subjective side. It is, rather, a unique combination of the subjective and the objective. Rooted in human needs and longings, it attempts to change the world. In hoping, we are pointing to an objective future that we wish to see happen, and anticipating that a certain state of affairs may come about. We act in the possibility that events may be smiling on us—that is, in circumstances in which our goals may actually be realized. Hope is neither a wholly subjective dimension of life nor a movement of events governed by iron laws. It is potency and possibility.

The kind of hope in trouble today is the stuff of the left. Those of us who have shared the experience of a social movement know all of the work that goes into it. But underneath the activity—and far less precise, even vague, and perhaps immeasurable—is the silent music that brings and keeps movements together, inspires them to keep going, and creates a sense of fellowship among their members. The sheer fact of acting collectively contains the hope of achieving specific and perhaps longer-range goals, and sometimes underpinning specific hopes is a wider and deeper common mood, a softer, shared spirit that links itself to other movements and their demands, past and present. Once that spirit is generated, it may wax and wane, but it never fades completely until a movement is crushed or it disperses.

The history of the modern West cannot be understood apart from such currents of hope. As Ernst Bloch describes it in his masterwork *Das Prinzip Hoffnung: The Principle of Hope*, only Marxism can realize what humans have hoped for throughout history. As he describes it, Marxism is both softly and deeply subjective, the "warm stream" in the most personal fantasies, and objective, the "cold stream" projecting concrete real-world possibilities. The two streams are intimately connected: historically, the "warm stream" was stirred by the growth of the "cold stream" of modern science and technology and the beginnings of industrialization, democratic revolutions, and secularization. But now, after Marxism, this "cold stream" no longer points to a better world, while the "warm stream" stands accused of illusions and false hopes.

It is striking that no scholar has written the story of hope, although histories of equally shifting, subjective, and ubiquitous attitudes have been attempted, including happiness, love, shame, guilt—and even hope's opposite, cynicism. After an early history characterized by ambivalence (the Greeks and Romans), a minor presence in the Hebrew Bible (a few mentions, especially in the Book of Job and the Psalms), hope becomes central in Christianity as the hope of beatitude with God in the afterlife. The revolutionary millenarianism of the end of the Middle Ages and the beginning of the modern period shows the first strong turn toward a hope that is both social and about life on earth.

And then comes the Enlightenment's full-throated and unreserved anticipation of our collective earthly future. It was best stated in Condorcet's *Sketch for a Historical Picture of the Progress of the Human Mind* and the writings of Marx. Condorcet based himself on the progress of science and the liberation of reason from authority and tradition. Marx rejected Comte's and Spencer's nineteenth-century notions of Progress as an autonomous force, insisting that creating a better world depended not only on material and technological progress, but above all on collective human struggle—involving consciousness, will, choice, strategy, and organization.

Both Marx and Condorcet helped shape the modern sense of hope. Describing it is a matter not of philosophical definition, but of historical recall. For all its particular forms and varieties, modern hope starts with a common sense of—to use Plato's language—*the good.* As Eric Hobsbawm describes it, all modernists stood on the "traditional ground of the classical humanist and liberal ideal. A world in which all were happy, and every individual fully and freely realized his or her potentialities, in which freedom reigned and government that was coercion had disappeared, was the ultimate aim of both liberals and socialists."[13] To be achieved, as David Caute says, through popular sovereignty[14]—or, as Geoff Eley describes it, by "forging democracy,"[15] it entails the possibility of all humans living freely and securely as equal citizens of democratic societies. Endowed with basic rights and liberties, all people would live without poverty, with the means to satisfy their fundamental needs, and with access to the education and leisure needed to fully develop their capacities. Obviously each of these aspects contains room for enormous disagreement, but more striking yet is the degree of agreement among the arguers. Even at the most contentious moments of the Cold War, for example, both sides claimed to share what had in fact become broad civilizational goals.

Entailed in this shared modern sense of the good is a sense of possibility: *It can be realized!* This confidence presupposes the existence of a critical mass of those who are, or who may become, agents bringing about desired change. Modern hope depends on a sense of collective human capacity. This presumes that people have the energy and will to carry out such a project: to understand it, to agree to it, to organize themselves to demand it, to do battle against those who oppose it, and to enact it when victorious. From the Enlightenment forward, then, modern hope has been characterized by a shared sense of the good, the *we* who can bring it about, the conviction that attaining it is possible, the will to act on it, and the capacity to achieve it. Hope is all of these elements combined, expressed in the attitude that *we can make the world better.*

It should be clear, then, why it is becoming urgent to talk about hope today. Its underlying premise, collective social and political action of a broad, sometimes even universal *we*, has become endangered. When politicians and parties in the United States, Britain, and Greece built campaigns around this theme of hope, and in Spain even named themselves Podemos—"We Can"—their confident-sounding assertions in fact were intended to counter the prevailing mood. They flew in the face of the widespread doubt that potential *we*'s still exist who are capable of acting effectively to bring about progressive democratic change. "Can we?" is the question they are trying to answer; "We can't" is the mood they are trying to throw off.

And, strange to say, they created a sense of possibility because they could see none all around them. Their organizing flew in the face of a widespread political passivity that seemed impossible to overcome. They were, and had to be, ringed by doubts. It no longer seems so clear that collective action can still produce meaningful positive results, or that social space exists for significant opposition. Moreover, it has become one staple of today's cynicism that unintended consequences inevitably undermine our intended results. Another is that leftist movements are incapable of functioning without huge doses of mythmaking and illusion, which inevitably generate discouragement. Indeed, perhaps democratic movements are incapable of effectively exerting collective intelligence and purpose. These doubts point to the unarticulated premises of all democratic movements of the last two centuries, which are now in question. Syriza has tried and capitulated, and it is because of and against these doubts that Podemos and the Sanders and Corbyn movements have been constructed.

It is not clear that collective social agency can still be effective in today's "individualized society," or where the neoliberal sea change has taken hold. Indeed, those who deny this kind of an active, collective subject and its "grand narrative" have become today's dominant voices. Social hope is in crisis today, and cynicism is riding high. When a movement like Syriza, with much of its leadership intact, can become the agent of neoliberal austerity, it is not surprising that skepticism should surround every step of the apparent breakthrough into the mainstream of a Bernie Sanders or a Jeremy Corbyn. Is this because a Donald Trump or a Nigel Farage can attract even more working-class voters than they frighten? Is it because the working class as the main social subject has given way to numerous other political identities? After all, these identities show no sign of coming together as a single, powerful force, and active citizenship has largely faded. Is this because neoliberalism has successfully, in Margaret Thatcher's formulation, "changed the soul" of the underlying population? Or is it because one-time citizens have become transformed into agglomerations of human capital? Is a society of citizens becoming a society of individuals, as Tocqueville warned might happen?

And who is the *we* anyway? Those in past democratic movements always knew what it meant to talk about "we," as did the New Left. Their demands, even where specific, were universal. Members of the second great wave of the women's movement, for example, had a clear sense of themselves as a core of activists advocating for and potentially including all women, with vast numbers of supporters, men as well as women, who understood that they were making revolutionary demands that were connected with other causes and would affect all of humanity. But, as I mentioned earlier, today many of those who continue to carry the torch of feminism do not see themselves or act as part of a larger movement. I would say "no longer see themselves" because they are historically and philosophically rooted in the New Left of the 1960s and 1970s. They contributed to and drank from the same broad current of social hope. As it receded, their specific constituency managed to keep the cause going by institutionalizing their specific demands and focusing away from the broader climate of oppression and liberation within which they emerged. Their *we* has become narrowed to one of among a dizzying plurality of *we*'s, each with its own agenda, some at each other's throats—or, worse, millions of distinct *I*'s, no longer able to generate any sense of a common good.

In today's climate, then, it is understandable that as Occupy Wall Street appeared, claiming to represent "the 99 percent," it was criticized for not really doing so, for being too young, too middle-class, too white, and too male. It is also understandable that Barack Obama's "hope" theme of 2008 sounds a little embarrassing to those who once participated in the exuberant movement-style wave that got its man elected and ended, pre-dictably, in disillusionment. For many, it wound up being experienced in retrospect as *we* acting collectively just enough to get *him* into office. Yet it is important to recall what "change you can believe in" meant in 2008 to those who became swept up in it, even momentarily: the Obama message tapped a genuine and, for some, even desperate longing generated by decades of conservative ideology and politics, years of the War on Terror, and then during the campaign the exploding of the housing bubble and the unfolding economic collapse.[16]

For all that onetime optimism, the Obama years only deepened the waning of hope that had been at work for a generation, and not only in the United States. As in the Mitterand years in France, new hopes were heralded, only to end in disillusionment and discouragement. Throughout the advanced world and especially in North America we have been living through a seismic shifting of expectations from the larger society to our own individual universes—the detaching of personal aspirations from the wider world. I call this the privatization of hope.

The 2010 movie *Waiting for Superman* eloquently expresses this current mood. Overlooked in the controversy provoked by the film—over charter schools, teachers' unions, and the role of poverty in determining educational outcomes—was its contribution to recasting hope in America. The film tracks five children, four of them inner-city African Americans or Hispanics in Harlem, the Bronx, Washington, DC, and East Los Angeles, whose parents are seeking a way out of the public schools. The four minority families see charter schools as their children's only chance. Where American public schools were once widely seen as providing a path to opportunity and

full citizenship, the film argues that they are drastically failing those who need them most, and that incompetent teachers, protected by their unions, are the main cause. Thus the
film leads us to its climax: five lotteries for charter school ad-
missions in various parts of the country, where our society's
winners and losers will be determined by lot. We have come
to identify with the five families, and we share their joy and
heartbreak. As the final credits roll, we are exhorted to "join the
movement."

Recipient of several awards, this film received financial
support from the world's richest man, Bill Gates, high praise
from President Obama, and a starring role on the *Oprah* television show. Historically, however, it may be judged rather differently, as forcefully documenting—and encouraging—the loss
of belief in public solutions to public problems. Its message
is that the public schools are unreformable, and that the best
solution for aspiring individual families is to escape them and
find their own way. In this it focuses and furthers the wider cultural process, the privatization of hope.

This odd-sounding formula is intended to call attention to
the fact that hope, like other social realities, has been recently
undergoing a sustained process of privatization. Today hope is
coming to be seen as a primarily individual, even psychological
matter concerning deeply held personal goals—such as real-
izing one's "dreams" in life or seeing one's children doing well.
To some extent this is due to the end of communism, since,
as Francis Fukuyama famously argued, we are now unable to
"picture to ourselves a world that is essentially different from
the present one, and at the same time better."[17] If we have
effectively reached the "end of history," this would mean that
the only remaining meaningful goals would be individual and

not social. History itself would have dictated the privatization of hope, by ending the urgency as well as possibility of major collective undertakings.[18] But of course this has not happened; what makes Fukuyama's claim absurd is that the great mass of humanity is nowhere near being able to "breathe easily."

Of course, the United States was always more individualistic than older European societies, because of the specific circumstances of its origins and growth. But this individualism eventually came to be complemented by a vast range of democratically decided collective projects: all the business of expansive federal, state, and local governments, and the provision of parks, schools, universities, libraries, health, public welfare, recreation, and even culture. Preserving and expanding many of these conditions came to be seen as ends in themselves: our collective goals, sources of pride, expressing our shared values.

These projects remind us of the remarkable shift the last generations have been living through. People are being taught to abandon social hope altogether, to become hostile to public projects and institutions. The notion of the common good is becoming replaced by a new individualism: crude, aggressive, and cynical. People seem increasingly unaware of having a social self. And so the "American Dream," whatever citizenship might have once meant to immigrant grandparents, seems to have narrowed today to an uninhibited pursuit of economic opportunity.

Certain causes of this waning of social hope have deep roots and have been widely discussed: the consumer society, the rise of the suburbs, the centrality of automobiles and television, the transformation of heavy industry and advent of the post-Fordist economy, the decline of trade unions and the rise of the "precariat," the prominence of the Internet, smartphones, and social media. Taken together, these trends suggest ways in which long-term transformations of our economic, political, social, and cultural landscape have been shaping a new kind of individual who knows little of collective experience and purposes and is oriented toward personal goals and satisfactions.

But other important trends are ambiguous, opening both toward greater social connectedness and greater individualization. People themselves, in movements demanding cultural, political, and social change—for free expression in poetry and music, for racial integration, for equality for women, for the acceptance of gays and lesbians, for multiculturalism—have opened up and enriched social and individual life simultaneously. Individuals are freer to become and share who they are as their social world becomes more respectful and tolerant of them. At the same time, we all live in "one world" as never before, and we experience a greater interdependency than ever, linking individuals with vast societal processes in a single global economy and society. No less ambiguous is the profusion of individually accessed electronic media. Technologies developed during this era have assumed a central role in our daily life such as cell phones, GPSes, MP3 players, smartphones, laptops, and tablet computers, along with the Internet and social media such as Facebook and Twitter. All of these are socially created devices that increase social interaction as well as individual power. In the 2011 demonstrations that momentarily seemed to transform Egypt and created the Occupy Wall Street movement, the social possibilities of the Internet and its devices became dramatically evident. What do we make of the fact that the new personal technologies, sometimes decried for isolating and separating individuals, also operate to connect people with each other and the wider world? While the various new technologies can contribute to the privatization of hope, they are themselves agnostic on the uses to which people put them. So if they do isolate and separate people, it is a result of their embeddedness in a prior scheme of political economy and social purposes.

Fully understanding today's privatization of hope means looking beyond recent historical and technological trends to a relentless political and ideological campaign over the last generation to draw people away from social concerns. The first mainstream ideologist of the renewed Hobbesianism was of course Margaret Thatcher: "There is no such thing as society, only individuals and families."

This mutation of what had previously been regarded as public themes into personal ones has thus been a deliberate, concerted project of politicians, economists, and ideologists, including those working for think tanks like the Cato and Heritage foundations. They have contributed much to the new individualism, imploring us to turn away from reshaping the public realm as a terrain for improvement and change, encouraging instead individual responsibility, personal initiative, and the centrality of private activities. It is no accident that for three years the only American protest movement responding to the Great Recession of 2008 was the Tea Party, calling for yet more of the very policies that had caused the crisis in the first place.

In the world of privatized hope, "markets," "choice," "economic freedom," and "individual liberty" are proclaimed as the simplest and clearest of truths. Passengers, participants, and students, all become "customers" as universities, nonprofits, and the entire world of culture are organized according to the same metrics as business firms. The transformation of social into individual hope is accompanied by massive cynicism toward any collective action not organized for profit. The fetish of market solutions for social problems is based on a revival of the faith, already obsolete at the beginning of the consumer society, that an invisible hand somehow coordinates millions of separate and competing activities.

But this is a fantasy that undermines our capacity to cope with the world's most urgent problems. How can people who experience themselves as separate, isolated individuals, lacking access to organized social action, ever find the wherewithal to master a threat such as climate change?[19] This cumulative effect of centuries of uncoordinated and separate actions can be controlled only if *we* accept that *we* have transformed nature and our relationship to it, and that humans have now become a geological force. Like it or not, it is urgent to acknowledge that human actions have generated the need for deliberate collective management of our interactions with nature. To protect our common home from disaster, humans must assert themselves as a universal global *we* that agrees on what must be done and how to do it. We must recover and enlarge social hope—in the name of survival.

Yet we have been becoming less and less politically, psychologically, and philosophically capable of doing so. The steadily progressing privatization of hope has been undermining the capacity for collective action. Precisely at the time when a major shift in human abilities, identities, and consciousness has become absolutely necessary, the disposition and ability to make such a shift has been under systematic assault. One source has been the denial generated by self-interested individuals and institutions. Another has been what Sartre calls *seriality*—the silence of passive, separated individuals. And yet another has been increasingly widespread cynicism, a disillusionment with collective action.

Certainly the Enlightenment, the industrial and French revolutions, modern societies and states—as well as the movements for slavery abolition, socialist revolution, and social-democratic reform and the struggles for national liberation and equal rights—have all carried their illusions with them. The passing of these waves has, little by little, engendered a sense of disillusioned hope and exhausted energy. But too much is being tossed aside by onetime liberals and social democrats disenchanted with the negative side effects of government action; by onetime radicals who feel defeated or betrayed by the desertions of many among them; by onetime technological utopians discouraged by the paltry social benefits of scientific progress; by baby boomers whose generational participation in ending the war in Vietnam was followed in time by one war after another, slowly morphing into today's endless war; and by those helplessly swept along by today's bottom line, who have "learned" that nothing can be done to soften the economic system's harshness. Powerful forces, both internal and external, have been telling us to be done with past illusions of bringing about change, and to adapt to and go along—to "face reality."

This conventional wisdom gives rise to the questions of this book: Is there reason to hope today? What kind of social hope remains viable today? Given our inevitable and justified post-Holocaust, post-communist, post-Marxist, post-Progress skepticism, what are the prospects for a reality-based social hope? What might it look like? For many, today seems to be characterized by an abundance of hope, a time of many activisms, with little sense of a meaningful alternative. Yet when the hope for *something else* seemed all but lost, Bernie Sanders and Jeremy Corbyn unexpectedly tapped that deep longing and shaped it into mainstream movements. How will hope be sustained in their aftermath? Indeed, how after Syriza's capitulation? Are there ways of understanding ourselves that strengthen the possibility of a global hope for the future? Beyond today's specific horizons of energy and enthusiasm, what realistic ways of thinking and acting point ahead?

In the end, this book is about seeing and experiencing things differently. If we are indeed living in a neoliberal world in which everything is organized in economic terms, in an "individualized society" that increasingly dictates "biographic solutions to systemic problems"—how to see our belongingness and power? How indeed, when almost everything conspires to separate us and confirm our impotence?

This book is an invitation to see ourselves living in the public, collective space where alone we can rediscover who we really are.

Chapter 2

What Hope Is

To hope is so many different things that no one knows quite how to think about it.[1] Speaking most simply and generally to hope is to have a positive expectation that a desired result may in fact come about. We do not quite look forward to or anticipate the result, because it is only possible; but we certainly point ourselves toward it. Hoping thus combines desiring with a sense of possibility, though not certainty. We hope when an outcome is in doubt, when it depends wholly or in part on conditions, forces, or people beyond our control. We may have contributed our own action, and we await results that may or may not be to our liking. Hoping, then, is looking forward to, but not counting on, a positive outcome.

We may hope passively or actively, collectively or individually, in fantasy or pragmatically, in a secular or a religious way, with close attention to realities and limits or with scant concern for them. Hoping might be passively waiting for the impossible to happen—or, despite a discouraging diagnosis, the conviction that "there's always something that can be done."

It can be praying to God to intervene. It can be encouraging others to join together in a political campaign, or counting on medical science to cure a disease. It can be anticipating any manner of good things happening, or morally trying to live in a way that God might favor. It can be arranging one's belongings on a concentration-camp bunk, or (in the case of Treblinka) plotting the near-impossible: to overcome the guards, burn down the camp, and escape. Hope can fill an African American church when the congregation and the choir sing an inspired hymn of praise that points beyond this world but shapes people's lives here and now. It can be, as in the American 1960s or the South African 1980s, participating in a movement for liberation. It can be as ordinary as waiting for an important phone call or sending out dozens of employment applications. Or, despite defeat and discouragement in a relationship, it can be a refusal to throw in the towel. It can involve taking a chance by talking union on the job—or it can be just waiting for a break in the weather. Or it can involve participating by demonstrating, signing a petition, contributing money, or just siding with one of a thousand campaigns that seek to save the rhinos, help immigrants, or assert that "black lives matter."

Hope is vague, hard to pin down, even irritating to those who insist on being realistic. The active verb form, "to hope," should be distinguished from "to have hope" because the constant talk about the latter betrays a current tendency to treat hope as a kind of quasi-thing that can be possessed, as something we can *have*, *obtain*, and *lose*. And both the active hoping and hope as something to be possessed can be distinguished from the state of mind that assumes that things will always work out for the best, or are currently working out no matter what we may do.

To hope is a peculiar stance, neither fish nor fowl, not quite an idea and not quite an attitude. Or it is all of these, but then also a mood, a feeling. It is an action that becomes a state of mind, or vice versa. Hope is vacuous and imprecise, yet whatever it is, it is clearly essential—inspiring people, motivating them, keeping them going in difficult times, even encouraging them to try an experimental treatment or to face brute force. Or it is the slender thread that remains when almost all is lost, as after the total destruction of Yiddishland, Jewish Eastern Europe, by the Nazis; Stalin's murder or deportation of tens of millions to Siberia; the Palestinian Nakba; the destruction of the Crow nation. Even worse, there are the times when the thread breaks completely, when hope is gone and all is lost.

A political movement dissipates as its members give up: they withdraw, wander off, abandon the struggle. They retreat into their individual selves. At times hope seems to be the highest good, but at other times we ridicule it as false and foolish. How to know the difference between the stubborn determination it encourages, and blind and self-destructive persistence? Refusing to give up hope demonstrates a force of will to keep on going. In thinking about hope, attention is most often paid to perseverance in the face of great odds, as is demonstrated by the fact that "the psychology of hope" generates many more times the number of Google hits than "the politics of hope." But hope is not only a soft, subjective attitude; it is an expectation that reaches beyond ourselves, and contains the wish and sometimes the determination to make something happen in the world.

One reason why hope is hard to pin down and is often ignored by activists is that its softness and subjectivity can embarrass those who are engaged in tough-minded social movements. While it underlies and accompanies and thus animates much of what we think and do, hope very rarely appears front and center as an object of direct attention. Instead, it usually resides within other ideas, feelings, and practices, needing to be teased out from them in order to be noticed. Elusive and unstable, hard to grasp, objective as well as subjective—no wonder it is so difficult to say what hope is.

How Not to Think about Hope

As we turn this kaleidoscope and constantly refocus on its ever-changing images of hope, we come across a way of viewing its shapes and colors all at once and all together. The 1,400 pages of Bloch's *Principle of Hope* present a striking perspective, seeing all images of satisfaction, from the humblest to the grandest, from the most intimately personal to the most broadly social, as flowing into a single stream, which is the meaning of human history. Bloch confidently asserts that this stream flows toward a better life, and that this becomes historically realizable only in the contemporary world as technological and social development make utopia possible. He contends that hope is everywhere and always of a single piece—singing a single song, if we only know how to interpret it.

Bloch's towering work reflects the urge to bring under Marxism's secular, sociopolitical projection of democracy, equality, and social justice, enriched by its halo of ages-old utopian longing, every conceivable hope humans have ever expressed. It is a breathtaking vision, seeking to unite all conceivable ways of projecting a better individual and collective existence, with hundreds of different kinds of longings and wishes and with the form and content of all art, in a unifying grand vision.

Bloch labored on this project from the 1930s to the 1950s, in exile in the United States and then in East Germany under the spell of Stalin's Soviet Union. The book points to the USSR as laying the basis for the fulfillment of humanity's deepest longings and fondest hopes. Bloch's political blindness about Soviet totalitarianism until he moved to the West in 1961 has its theoretical counterpart in his intellectual determination to bring all wishes, images, and longings under a single totalizing rubric. After all, many of humanity's hopes are not ultimately political, nor do they all lead to political action. The problem is that the hopes Bloch describes include much that is strictly individual and personal (daydreams of love, for example), and much that is broadly civilizational (images of the kind of integral gratification that are intrinsically limited by all reality principles), as well as much that is totally unrealizable (images of everlasting life, for example). Many of the expressions of hope catalogued by Bloch are too extensive to be encompassed by any sociopolitical order; indeed, many of them imply no world-improving sociopolitical action at all. Many do not even imply action, and are not even anticipation, but are poignant wishes for the unattainable (a return to youth, for example). Indeed, how much of longing remains passive, resigned to not having one's object in this life, or indeed is hopeless?

But if Bloch, like Stalinism, confuses hope by allowing no space for the strictly private and personal, recent thinkers do the opposite. Currents and movements of collective hope are not among the dozens of kinds of hope surveyed in Terry Eagleton's *Hope without Optimism*. In many ways, Eagleton's book might be regarded as an anti-Bloch treatise, given its attack not only on Bloch's extravagances but equally on his optimism, as well as for its most significant thread, Eagleton's explorations of the wisp of hope that remains after defeat and destruction. But how do movements, cultures, and societies generate hope in the first place and sustain it, and how do they actively pursue goals? What is social hope? Determined to avoid buying hope "on the cheap," or the empty optimism he spends a chapter demolishing, Eagleton is instead preoccupied with the "fundamental hope" that "survives the general ruin"—his major examples including Gabriel Marcel's reflections during the German Occupation of France and the last lines of Shakespeare's *King Lear*. Eagleton begins his final chapter, "Hope against Hope," with the bracing example, drawn from Jonathan Lear's *Radical Hope*, of the Crow tribe's last great chief: "As the case of Plenty Coups illustrates, the most authentic kind of hope is whatever can be salvaged, stripped of guarantees, from a general dissolution. It represents an irreducible residue that refuses to give way, plucking its resilence from an openness to the possibility of unmitigated disaster."[2]

These are essential analyses for anyone concerned with salvaging hope from disaster, as we all must be in the wake of the catastrophic twentieth century.[3] For the most part, however, Eagleton explores hope as the expression of an abstract subject, the generalized individual of most of the hundreds of literary and philosophical sources on which his book is based. Although he touches at one point on "performative" hope and at another on the hopes of the left, he barely registers the kinds of hope that have emerged in the modern world as concrete individuals have come together to act collectively for social and political purposes. Despite the dozens of hopes he sifts through in his "What Is Hope?" chapter, Eagleton is not interested in the historical shift that takes place at the beginning of the modern world as a *we* takes shape that begins to hope actively, in collective and secular ways, for a better world. While his book exudes the sense of hope being in trouble today, he never concretely and specifically asks why that is.

Social hope is absent as well from Patrick Shade's more concrete and activist *Habits of Hope*. Shade's pragmatic theory explores in fine detail how hopeful attitudes can become implanted and sustained in the self. But he does not see that self collectively, as belonging to processes that demand more than merely adding selves. Toward the end of the book he gestures briefly toward "communities of hope," but these never become concrete or historical, taking no notice of the fact that hoping together in communities gives hope a new shape. Shade's study of individual hope never turns toward the kinds of hope that actually take place in a community.

There is, however, an important way in which Shade does help us think about hope fruitfully, which is the main thrust of his book. A pragmatic theory of hope regards it as "the active commitment to the desirability and realizability of a certain end." Trying to focus discussions on how individuals can learn to act on and realize our hopes, Shade spells out daily attitudes and skills, personal "habits of hope," that might allow the selves he is concerned with to function hopefully and effectively at the same time.[4] But, like Eagleton, he leaves us with the impression that social hope is nothing more than individual hope writ large. In turning the kaleidoscope, however, we see social hope as a unique species of hope with a very specific shape and coloration. As individuals come together in collective action, a new kind of hope is born. Collective efforts to achieve practical social goals generate ways of thinking, experiencing, perceiving, and acting that are inaccessible to the single individual. My hope, or hope in general, is not like *our* hope, the hope of the *we*.

Guides to Thinking about Social Hope

A surprising source of tools for thinking about social hope is the work of Jean-Paul Sartre. This is unexpected because of the individualism of Sartre's basic terms and the difficulties his thought encounters in lacking the social dimension demanded by his political commitments. But at one decisive moment in his career, Sartre the individualist considers how social struggle takes shape; this is when the series becomes a group in *Critique of Dialectical Reason*. Sartre talks about the phenomenon of seriality: socially imposed arrangements in which each of us acts alongside others, but in isolation from them. Waiting for a bus in an orderly queue is one example, listening to the Top Forty is another. This state of *us*ness, of a passive and externally determined collectivity, is our customary social experience, whose outer limits we reach in highly charged but still serial moments of national tragedy, sporting events, and elections. In his discussion of seriality in the *Critique*, Sartre points out that the state of separation and passivity may break down under conditions of threat or need. If the bus doesn't show up, we may form ourselves into a group trying to do something about the situation. The hope I am talking about begins there.[5]

As the group takes action, we return to the thought of Ernst Bloch, this time for guidance. The specifically modern hope

I am concerned with is not simply subjective desire, Bloch's "warm stream." It also includes the "cold stream" of social and political reality, focusing on the practical intention of making objective changes and being guided by real-world considerations. Social hope, the disposition to act collectively to change a situation, entails that we act not blindly but with a sense of possibility. The cold stream demands that we prepare ourselves and assess the conditions under which we are operating. The hope of social movements calls for objective, clearheaded organization and action, and an appreciation of the circumstances in which we may be successful. This realistic stream of hope mingles with the visionary stream that motivates us; without both, there is no hope. Hope uniquely combines our longing, our own real intention, and our sense of potency with real possibility, the subjective and the objective.

For Bloch, as hope enters the modern age, its ultimate horizon is utopia, which becomes a realistic possibility for the first time in history. His is a vision from the left, projecting a specific, secular sociopolitical hope for a classless society that embodies democracy, equality, and social justice. He would not deny that looking elsewhere, we can find less appealing social hopes: to protect or to assert privilege, to create our own community and exclude or dominate others, to deny freedoms or rights, to reject the very notion of community. But to Bloch, modern social hope is driven and enriched by age-old longings, and it reaches out to everyone with its vision of a universal community where all share well-being. Thus there would no doubt be something self-contradictory, internally compromised, about a social hope that would shrink its vision, limiting, restricting, or excluding other people's hopes.

The contemporary who grasps this hope better than anyone

is not a philosopher or theorist but a self-described "writer, historian, and activist," Rebecca Solnit. Two of her books, *A Paradise Built in Hell* and *Hope in the Dark*, are rooted in a double sense: "This is an extraordinary time full of vital, transformative movements that could not be foreseen. It's also a nightmarish time."[6] The worst nightmares, past and present, give rise to collective responses that express the best in people: 9/11, Hurricane Katrina, the San Francisco earthquake, and dozens of disasters and horrible conditions that mobilize people, drawing them out of isolation, passivity, and cynicism. Solnit has in mind all of the many currents usually gathered under the label "left," but stresses equally changes in ideas, values, forms of interaction, and local and small-scale practices, all of which may simmer beneath the surface for years and only occasionally burst out as noticeable political movements.

Hope in the Dark takes the form of a series of mini-lectures to activists that aim at strengthening hope by educating them in how to see themselves, their attitudes, their activity, and the width, breadth, and depth of their results. Solnit seeks "to propose a new vision of how change happens; I want to count a few of the victories that get overlooked; I want to assess the wildly changed world we inhabit; I want to throw out the crippling assumptions that keep many from being a voice in the world."[7] In doing so, she stresses how much has changed and how unexpectedly it has changed, how to avoid "false hope and easy despair," and the need to count victories in all their variety. She stresses above all that hope is social, and that it arises in action.

As Bloch, Sartre, and Solnit discuss social hope, then, they are specifically concerned with movements of the left. Modern social hope has posed the broad goal of an equal and democratic society of plenty, as well as at various moments such specific goals as labor unions, parliamentary government, universal suffrage, an end to slavery, an end to foreign and colonial rule, and the inclusion of workers' and labor parties in positions of power. Further goals have included reducing or even ending economic inequality, ending poverty, creating old-age security, making education and medical care freely available to all, and equalizing opportunity, as well as expanding rights and ending racial, gender, and sexual inequality. Alongside this standard list of concerns has risen a panoply of more recent issues, many of them far more specific, concerning indigenous peoples, ethnic groups, religious minorities and nonbelievers, and subcategories of workers, often under the rubric of "rights," as well as the broad movement against climate change and its many specific movements, including those against pipelines, fracking, and toxic waste dumps. All these add up to what Solnit celebrates as a "vast, inchoate, nameless movement—not a political movement but a global restlessness, a pervasive shift of imagination and desire—that has recently appeared in almost every part of the world."[8]

In all these respects I am in total agreement with Solnit. And this book resembles her work in a more basic way: it is not a reflection on hope from a distance, but rather is written, echoing Marge Piercy, "from the Movement, for the Movement." But while I share Solnit's sense of excitement about the energies for resistance and change bubbling up all around us, I am equally concerned with hope in trouble, the *loss* of hope over the last generation and its causes. What follows is a discussion of how social hope takes shape. The next chapter will explore how the maelstrom of "growth" and "development" is at war with social hope. Chapter 4 will discuss the cynicism that infects our society. And in chapter 5, I will explore today's trend for social hope to become privatized as social goals become transmuted into personal ones. Chapter 6 then returns to Solnit and explores the continuing sources of social hope despite these trends. In solidarity with Solnit, then, what follows here is not so much a book *about* hope as it is a book *of* hope.

The We *behind Social Hope*

My main intent in what follows is to tease out what happens individually and collectively as movements of the left generate and sustain social hope. This kind of "progressive" social hope is not confined to movements; it can take many forms, including political parties, labor unions, single-issue advocacy groups, insurgent electoral campaigns, and foundations. These may achieve stability as top-down institutions with paid staff, permanent offices, and complex organizations financed by grants or sophisticated fundraising apparatus. These ways of institutionalizing social hope can at times display some of the essential features and structures of a movement for social hope—especially during drives to win elections, lobby governments, pressure corporations, or promote legislation. This happens, for example, as organizations campaign on behalf of specific human rights such as gay marriage, to protect specific aspects of the environment such as rivers or lakes, or to save particular endangered animals such as black rhinos or California condors.

Social hope starts with the fact that its subject is collective: *we* and not *I*. It is not just any *we*; in one way or another, the *we*'s are at work forging, expanding, and deepening democracy.[9] In coming together and collectively articulating goals, we posit them as values, goods to be achieved. When we contest existing societal arrangements, such objectives of collective hope necessarily become justified morally. Valued and desired, these goals are also *willed*: we mobilize to make them happen. Of course such mobilization depends on our collective strength and capacity, and although we cannot presuppose this with full confidence, we know that it will have to be demonstrated by our efforts. But it also turns out that in our hopeful action we must depend not only on ourselves, but on various forces in the wider world. And, to an important extent, history must smile on our project: it must be a realistic possibility. Of course we may not know until afterwards whether a particular hope was realistic—whether it be to achieve collective bargaining, to end apartheid, or to end segregation. A key feature of hoping is to project as achievable what has often been rejected as "unrealistic."[10]

Value, will, capacity, and possibility: in thus moving from the warm stream to the cold, hope comes to life. It begins with a *we*, individuals coming to see themselves acting as part of a larger collectivity. But what kind of collectivity is it, since *we* is not the same as *us*? Jean-Paul Sartre talks about the phenomenon that might be described as *us*ness, which he calls seriality—socially imposed arrangements in which each of us acts alongside others but in isolation from them. Waiting for a bus in an orderly queue is one example, listening to the Top Forty is another. The state of *us*ness, of a passive and externally determined collectivity, is our customary social experience, whose outer limits we reach in highly charged but still serial moments of national tragedy, sporting events, and elections. In the thought experiment that is the *Critique of Dialectical Reason*,

Sartre points out that the state of separation and passivity may break down under conditions of threat or need. If the bus doesn't show up, we may form ourselves into a group trying to do something about the situation. The hope I am talking about begins there. Or it begins with a few workers grumbling about their working conditions, when one of them suggests that maybe they "should do something about it," and someone else agrees to get together to talk further. Or it begins when someone contacts a group of friends and neighbors about organizing a community meeting to discuss the impending war, and then they set a date and reserve a room at the local library for a meeting.

Large collectivities that seek to bring about significant change are called *movements,* as in great masses of people marching toward the seat of government. They move together and deliberately toward achieving a common political, economic, or social goal, often aiming at recasting prevailing relations of power. For over two centuries the constantly assembling, fragmenting, and regathering *we*'s of the left have done this, generating, contributing to, and inspired by the hope to create a better world.

Being and Perceiving as We

A movement exists in order to bring about certain changes, and in the process of participating or identifying with it, we change in both our being and our perception. This is both an ontological and an epistemological transformation. We become members of a larger entity, drawing power from it, having responsibility to it, and experiencing ourselves within it. Our active, collective stance generates a sense that it is possible to alter social reality, and so recasts situations and relationships that have seemed to be fixed and blocked. The very existence of a *we* overcomes the passivity in which its members have found themselves before bringing it into being. By contesting existing social structures and practices, the *we* demands that things be more fair, more humane, more equal, more democratic. We thus challenge the dominant system of power, those who benefit from it, and those who control it. In so acting, we sense the possibility of things being different, and we experience our own power to make it so. Self-empowered, we willingly contest those in power. Solidarity—each for each other, all for each, and each for all—replaces individual self-seeking as our social norm. And we draw upon and contribute to a new current of aspirations and morality. This can eventually become wider than our own *we* and our own specific demands, and can be seen to stretch back in time and to shape our present, as well as forecasting a better future for everyone. In creating ourselves as a movement, then, we create hope.

This remarkable change in our being is accompanied by a no less remarkable change in our perception. By becoming collective actors opposing ourselves to other actors, we look for their weaknesses and resistances as well as our own strengths and the objective possibilities of change. The once fixed and frozen field before us becomes redefined as our practical one, and once we become its active agents, our adversaries lose their apparent autonomy, their quality of givenness. We analyze them in terms of their purposes, strengths, and vulnerabilities. The complex historical and social field is no longer simply an immovable fact of life, but now becomes a series of guides, helps and obstacles. Once viewed individually and passively, formerly overwhelming forces now become antagonists to be overcome or circumvented. Once-fixed situations are now experienced as being fluid and subject to change. This may be a psychological change, but the change in how we see is also a change in *what* we see. We recognize social arrangements, "the way things are," as humanly created—and look for the ways to change them.

The Power of We

To continue the thought experiment, imagine or recall what it is like, this *we* of a movement. I will refer frequently to a few specific movements over the past century: the Paterson Silk Strike of 1913; the Flint sit-down strike of 1936–37; the long, complex, and many-sided movements for civil rights in the United States; the even longer, more complex, and infinitely varied struggles against apartheid in South Africa; and Occupy Wall Street. Within such efforts, or even among those who support or sympathize with them, I change by entering their *we*. I experience a new sense of possibility. My own horizon now widens beyond myself: the *we* becomes a locus of perception and engine of action, engaged in changing the situation.

To a skeptic with no memory of such an experience or ability to imagine it, it may sound implausible that the impotence of scattered individuals can give way to an empowered sense of *we*. It may seem far-fetched that the formerly powerless can generate something new, social hope, by acting together. Cynicism about such possibilities has become a dominant attitude of our time, and I will explore this phenomenon in depth in chapter 4. But for the moment I would answer the skeptic by recalling some images that speak for themselves. On YouTube we can witness Nelson Mandela's walk to freedom on February 11, 1990, after twenty-seven years in prison, and then his speech in Cape Town that evening, in which he began by thanking specific individuals and organizations in South Africa and around the world who had made his release possible. We can also see the electrifying images from four years later of newly empowered citizens standing in long lines to vote in the first free South African elections. These were moments of high drama that redefined the world's sense of what was possible.

There have been other dramatic times when everything has seemed to come together: of a collective will, its power, and the sense of expectation it has generated. One such moment was the early morning of December 5, 1955, in Montgomery, Alabama, when the buses rolled from black neighborhoods to the rest of the city completely empty. *We* assembled together in the evening, in church. But *we* were much more powerfully present in the empty buses, in the knots of people walking to work and home, in the car pool vehicles carrying people around the city. On the evening of June 7, 1913, many of us were onstage in the Pageant, in which Paterson Silk workers enacted the story of their strike in drama and music before an overflow crowd of fifteen thousand at Madison Square Garden in New York.

Such electrifying events capture, in especially striking ways, the spirit and meaning of a movement. In response to skeptics who stress, correctly, how short-lived these moments are, it is worth pointing out that each one has been imbedded in a patient struggle, belonging to a longer and not always happy story. The Montgomery bus boycott sprang from a long line of similar disobedient actions that stretch back to slave rebellions and the Underground Railroad, and which include organizing sources such as the Marcus Garvey movement and the NAACP. The bus boycott wore on for thirteen months in 1955–56, and in any case its victory only presaged the struggles to come. The Paterson Silk strikers belonged to a wave of labor insurgency instigated by the Industrial Workers of the World (IWW), and they managed to hold out for five months before their strike collapsed. The South African events are rooted in a history that dates back at least to the beginning of the African National Congress in 1912, its Defiance Campaign in 1952, and its armed struggle beginning in 1961.

The stirring events of 1990 and 1994 should not blind us to the many disappointments of what Martin Murray calls "the painful birth of postapartheid South Africa,"[11] but they should also remind us of a decisive reason why social hope is so often able to sustain itself under great duress and over long periods of time. Movements are sustained by the slow accretion of successes, each of which demonstrates and thereby reinforces the sense of the movement's power. Empty buses and stores, shut down factories, silent township schools, "whites only" and "colored only" signs removed—these are collective perceptions seen together through thousands of eyes, shared and talked about and experienced together, all feeding and testifying to the strength of mass movements.

This phenomenon is perceived as both negative and positive power, in what we have done and what we have brought to a halt. In South Africa it was demonstrated spectacularly by the 1980–81 attacks on oil refineries, power stations, and military and police installations. These attacks were part of the Umkhonto we Sizwe guerilla campaign, which aimed at giving heart to the internal opposition to apartheid and showing the ANC's destructive capacity, although it was never intended as a vehicle for assuming power. It was a visible reply to the South African state, which had amassed enormous military power capable of crushing any internal dissent or guerilla movement, as well as by 1982 acquiring its first atomic bomb. This military might had shallow foundations: by 1980 whites were only 16 percent of the population, while Africans, Indians, and coloreds together made up 84 percent. However this demographic fact might be perceived by single, separated individuals, it registered in movement eyes, was collectively discussed, and was a core reason not only for the majority movement's sense of right, but also for its ultimate self-confidence that asserting itself politically, economically, and even militarily would eventually bring down apartheid.

Thus it had to be powerfully encouraging that the government scrapped the program of Afrikaans-language education after the Soweto uprising of 1976, and that during the upheavals of the 1980s it scurried to do away with "petty apartheid" forms of segregation while creating a new constitution that included minor forms of political consultation and even representation for nonwhites. None of these moves could placate the great mass of Indians, coloreds, and Africans, but in fact they only increased the self-confidence of the movement in its demand for political power and the complete end of apartheid.

African Americans could have no such demographic self-assurance. They were a massive presence in the South, but were nevertheless a minority outside "Black Belt" counties. And in the country as a whole, they were only 10 percent of the population. From the beginning, then, the campaign to end segregation in the United States lacked the South Africans' demographic self-confidence in ultimate victory. Segregation was deeply imbedded socially, economically, and politically, and it constantly reflected to black people their own powerlessness. The movement contested this locally in a thousand places and ways, including early dramatic campaigns to desegregate lunch counters and bus travel, but activists always knew that they were ultimately dependent on federal intervention, and therefore on the goodwill of a majority of whites nationally. In part, then, African Americans' power had to be moral. They hoped to arouse the conscience of Northern whites, and thus the White House. At the same time, all the arrests, trials, and convictions, as well as all the beatings, shootings, and murders, were unable to stop the movement's appeal beyond Southern towns and cities, or to keep Southern towns and states from yielding one concession after another. Each national broadcast or telecast or newspaper article, each local concession, each federal intervention only further fueled the hopes of people in the movement.[12]

Taking Charge of Our Lives

There is another side to the sense of power at the heart of social hope. These are times, and historians can point to many of them, when individuals acting together are engaged in the process, in Steve Golin's words, of "actively taking charge of their own lives."[13] One senses that this happened in the complex and tenacious self-organization of the Montgomery Bus boycott, in which thousands of African Americans replaced the public transportation system that took them to work and to shopping but humiliated them every time they boarded a bus. From a few privately owned cars, they created a massive system of sharing rides that lasted for thirteen months, even though the city harassed it and declared it illegal. This taking charge happened during the Paterson strike, and unskilled immigrant Italians and Jews and skilled English silk workers overcame their differences and forged a remarkable unity. During the 1980s civic associations were generated in the South African townships that carried out boycotts and rent strikes. In such times, as Golin says of Paterson, the movements became "a way of life," developing complex organizations, generating and drawing on new talents, creating new patterns of living, opening up new possibilities for ordinary people, inspiring—and needing—their ingenuity, sacrifice, and even heroism.

Flint

In Flint, Michigan in late 1936, the United Automobile Workers (UAW) decided to organize a strike, following the example of the successful French strike wave earlier that year, in order to achieve union recognition by General Motors. In describing the "sit-down community" in Flint, Sidney Fine gives us a sense of how separate individuals came together as a *we* in action, generating hope as they did. The strikers organized "little governments" in their plants, with committees "for every conceivable purpose": "food, recreation, information, education, postal services, sanitation, and contact with the outside."[14] They created rules and a judicial system (with punishments for infractions), and organized musical entertainment. Outside the plants, "a network of committees was created in Flint to support the strike in all of its aspects: defense (protection), sound cars, picketing, transportation, welfare, kitchen (food), publicity, organization, entertainment, information, education, distribution, car repairs and gas, finances, hall sanitation, speakers bureau, women's auxiliary, and war veterans."[15] Although the strikers were away from their homes and under constant strain, they, "almost for the first time, became acquainted with one another and began to develop a sense of fellowship and coherence. There was, during the strike, a 'greater sociability,' a recognition of a 'consciousness of kind,' a feeling of solidarity produced by the common struggle in which the strikers were engaged. 'It was like we were soldiers holding the fort,' one of the Chevrolet No. 4 sit-downers declared. 'It was like war. The guys with me became my buddies.' "[16]

How, then, did hope operate in Flint? A small, coherent leadership group initiated the action, attracted others, and galvanized enough workers to seize and hold the plant. Supporters mobilized on the outside, including UAW officials sent to Flint to help, nonstriking workers, the Women's Emergency Brigade, members of strikers' families, and the wider community. A national network of support was organized, creating and spreading publicity and lobbying government officials. All of these became part of the wider *we* who participated.

Any story of this great event is radically incomplete that does not include the major role played by the organized left. This is described by the wife of one striker and daughter-in-law of another, Socialist Party activist Genora Johnson Dollinger, who created the Women's Emergency Brigade. She tells about Flint's numerous left networks in the period, which included the Socialist Party, the Communist Party, the Proletarian Party, the Socialist Labor Party, and the League for Industrial Democracy. These groups—and then, starting in 1936, the UAW—organized among Flint's communities of autoworkers, which included local workers and those drawn from Michigan farms, migrants from the South, miners from the copper and iron range up north, Russians, Poles, Scots, and Scandinavians, as well as older hands who had been part of the IWW. Despite the fear and conformity pervading a city dominated by the General Motors Corporation, during the 1930s left organizations had distributed newspapers, held classes and discussion groups, and presented speakers, giving Flint autoworkers essential theoretical bearings and organizational experience.[17]

Many, indeed most, GM workers in Flint were not members of the UAW—the sit-ins were the tactic of a small minority working closely together. But this minority was not made of soldiers commanded from on high. For example, the daring seizure of Chevrolet plant no. 4 on February 1, 1937, broke the stalemate and led directly to the settlement ten days later. Fine points out that it was "the local Flint leadership rather than the UAW international officers or CIO officials who were primarily responsible for initiating and implementing the 'gamble' that in the end played such a large part in determining the outcome of the strike."[18]

Self-organization, solidarity, the ingenuity of ordinary people: however momentarily, people live differently and become different. This is precisely what happened in the Occupy movements, which, while they lasted, created functioning oppositional communities in full view and on public space. They rejected the importance of leadership, and operated according to new forms of participatory democracy.

Hope Becomes Contagious

The career of Occupy Wall Street and its offshoots dramatically shows a further feature of hope: it can become contagious as movements encourage other movements. Our sense of possibility may depend on our seeing that others are acting on behalf of similar goals. Inspired in part by the various demonstrations of the Arab Spring in early 2011, activists met in August to plan Occupy Wall Street. It was not only successful beyond their wildest expectations, but it spread around the world like wildfire. Every American city of any size saw similar encampments, all clearly part of the same national and then international movement. People halfway around the earth strongly affect those who would do something similar here, crystallizing the will to act. They give us hope. Inspired by them, we now think that we can do likewise, and that our situation is as ripe for change as is theirs.

In 1912 the textile workers' victory in the "Bread and Roses" strike (so named because the workers' protest signs read "We want bread but roses too!") in Lawrence, Massachusetts, certainly encouraged Paterson silk workers. Lawrence gave them a new sense of their own power and of what was possible if they used it. And when the Lawrence IWW leadership agreed to come to Paterson to help them, why should they not have expected a similar result?

Similarly, the 1936 sit-downs in France, which led to the Popular Front government and a wave of reforms, encouraged UAW activists to try the tactic in the United States. Closer to home, rubber workers in Akron prodded and inspired auto workers in Michigan. Dollinger summarized the response in Flint: "If they can do it, why can't we? . . . And how can we do it?"[19] Other events smiled on their project: the overwhelming success of Roosevelt and the Democrats in the 1936 elections, the election of Frank Murphy as governor of Michigan, and the consolidation of most auto workers in a single industrial union, along with the defeat of the craft-oriented American

Federation of Labor by the new Congress of Industrial Organizations in elections for its leadership. A new situation, a new tactic, the militants now in control of the union, the example of others' bold action and victory, the sense that we were not alone—these combined in 1936 and 1937 to generate the hope that this time the auto plants could be organized.

Since the promising "moment of 1913" there have been at least five anni mirabiles, times when enthusiastic waves of movement-centered social hope spread around the world: 1917–23, 1936–37, 1968, 1989, and 2011. At each of these times, activists in one place attempted a new course of action, made demands, unified themselves into a more or less coherent group, attracted large numbers, and soon found themselves leading an enormous mass movement. Then others elsewhere picked up the baton. As Fine points out, the GM strike spurred a wave of sit-down strikes throughout American industry, involving "every conceivable type of worker—kitchen and laundry workers in the Israel-Zion Hospital in Brooklyn, pencil makers, janitors, dog catchers, newspaper pressmen, sailors, tobacco workers, Woolworth girls, rug weavers, hotel and restaurant employees, pie bakers, watchmakers, garbage collectors, Western Union messengers, opticians, and lumbermen."[20]

South Africans, at it far longer than anyone, experienced the hope and inspiration that come from seeing one's cause elsewhere by witnessing the independence of black Africa starting with Ghana in 1957, by hearing about the American civil rights movement winning major victories against segregation during the 1960s, and by seeing nearby Mozambique and Angola become liberated from Portugal in the 1970s and hold on against South African– and American-supported insurgencies in the 1980s. At the same time they gained hope from the support of what grew to be a worldwide anti-apartheid movement not only expressing solidarity with their struggle but demanding that their governments impose sanctions on the apartheid government and businesses investing in South Africa.

We *Reconsidered*

The *we* that forms in such situations of social hope is not something mystical or magical. Nor is it a hyperorganism, a self-sustaining being moving on its own beyond the individuals who make it up. But like many another collective entity—an army, the state, a tribe, a nonprofit, the United Nations—it is more than the sum of its parts, mustering new powers in being created, able to perform feats that are otherwise unthinkable. And yet more than most of these others, it is fragile, held together by the volition of its members, capable of dissolving when that is withdrawn.

Sartre points out that shortly after forming themselves into a group, the members of that group feel the need to pledge themselves to it in order to sustain it beyond that moment. This act of consolidation happens freely and spontaneously, but the collective decision begins to impose a weight on the members, including responsibility for maintaining the collectivity and sanctions for failing to do so. So begins the practice and process of the group's institutionalization. In thus working on the group itself, a stable leadership will be created and will assert the group members' imperatives on each other and everyone else. For Sartre, this is the process through which a revolutionary group passes for the sake of its survival, becoming ever more rigid, and even eventually becoming a dictatorship.

Without following all the steps of Sartre's analysis in the second half of the *Critique*, we can see clearly that the *we* of a movement is not necessarily the spontaneous coming together of individuals who find themselves at the same place at a given moment, or with the same needs or the same consciousness of what must be done. It may rather be the more or less deliberate product of a team actively planning for months or years, as with the demonstrations in Tahrir Square, Egypt, or the coming together of smaller coherent groups at the right moment, such as those who planned the Flint sit-down strike at General Motors in 1936–37.

Unity becomes a key theme of such movements, because it is never a given and often has to be forged over time, and because the tendency to fragment is so strong. The South African and US civil rights struggles went on for years, each with many leaderships competing, movements constantly recomposing and disintegrating, and would-be leading organizations in constant disagreement and discouraged by tactical and strategic mistakes, yet without ever losing a strong degree of coherence, energy, and will. Obviously, then, individuals and contending groups may have sharply different interests and perceptions not only of movement goals, but of what to do and how to do it.

Accordingly a *we*, this locus of hope, is always a work in progress, and keeping it together is as essential as the movement's outward thrust. How does its unity come about in the first place? The 1913 Paterson strike was a general strike against the entire silk industry in its national center, and it included ribbon weavers, loom operators, and dyers' helpers—workers with different skills, pay scales, and histories of union struggle who belonged to different ethnic groups and were not accustomed to cooperating with each other. It was, in fact, a remarkable

feat of the strike to bring highly skilled and long-rooted weavers from England together with poorer, less skilled, and more
recently arrived Jews and Italians. And these workers, represented by different unions, reached out to the famously radical
IWW for help after they had led the workers in Lawrence to
victory.

In South Africa the situation was drastically different. Unlike Paterson and Flint, South Africa is a single vast country,
with a land mass greater than Germany and France combined
and a population of sixteen million people in 1960 and nearly
forty million by the first free election in 1994. It is so geo-
graphically and ethnically diverse that even thinking in terms
of a single South African people is a considerable feat of the
imagination. The African National Congress, originally a movement of middle-class Africans, eventually came to unite under
its nonracialism Africans, Indians, mixed-race coloreds, and
liberal and left-wing whites, and then in the 1980s the great
mass of the labor movement. In doing so, it contested black
nationalists who were also opposed to apartheid, and groups
representing a great variety of ethnic, economic, and regional
interests, as well as those fostered by government policies in
the pseudoindependent homelands and the quasiautonomous
Zulu regions in Natal.

Involved in successive waves of intense activism in the
1950s and early 1960s, the ANC was effectively repressed by
being banned and its leadership imprisoned. There followed
a long spell of quietism, broken by the Soweto uprising in
1976, which saw thousands of young people flee the country,
many of whom became part of the ANC's guerilla apparatus.
By the mid-1980s a huge wave of unrest had broken out again,
and ANC loyalists and competing activists formed vast net-

works of local movements demanding many different things and operating on different levels. Divided by many different hopes, these movements were also united by a common one: to end white majority rule. In this specific aim, the ANC and its leadership in prison and exile operated as the pole star of the widest imaginable *we*. In this sense, then, there was a single, if always contested, movement—resisting massive government repression, laboring amidst enormous complexity and constant internal conflict, inspiring battles on many fronts, and creating its own deep and widespread alternative culture.

Perhaps the most creative effort to form a *we* was that of the Occupy movements: "We are the 99 percent." The slogan was formulated by a movement that was based on no specific identity of class, race, gender, or ethnicity. With these words mostly young, mostly under- or unemployed, mostly college-educated occupiers managed to reach out widely, in ways that included winning support from labor unions and individual union activists. They briefly created the sense that the vast majority of Americans (and people in other Occupy countries) shared the same interests and resentments and were dominated by a tiny minority—"the 1 percent" who controlled political power and the global economy. Thus, *we* was in part actually present in the encampments and in part symbolic. Once its actual participants, a few tens of thousands, were driven out of their encampments, the movement mostly disbanded. In so doing, it left behind, in the United States at least, a new public concern about inequality and the power of the very wealthy over government, and a movement experience that would be rekindled during the Bernie Sanders presidential campaign.

In contrast, the *we* of the Flint sit-down strike became institutionalized in the UAW, and that of the dominant ANC wing of the anti-apartheid movement became transformed into South Africa's governing party. The Paterson strikers were at a constant disadvantage because the courts and police operated on behalf of the mill owners, and the mill owners were able to move production to unorganized mills in Pennsylvania. After five months, the strikers could no longer raise enough financial support to feed themselves and their families. Their unity collapsed and they gave in to the pressure to go back to work, either individually or by separate union decisions. The *we* dissolved, or at best some of its component unions settled separately, and the strike ended.

Yes We Can

The core of every movement's hope can be summarized by a profound expression that was turned into one of the most hackneyed slogans of recent political memory. A generation ago, Latino farmworkers in the American Southwest organized themselves under the slogan "Si se puede"—the original "Yes we can." *We*, acting together, can overcome skepticism and cynicism, mobilize our collective power, combat those forces discouraging and oppressing us, and transform our situation. Each element of the phrase is tied to the others. "Yes" is an answer to the implicit "no" that is our starting point: the "no" of those who say we cannot act effectively, that it won't make a difference. It is also the "no" of a passive us, of individuals scattered and separate even while working and living alongside each other, unable to make a difference in our common condition. But "we can" means that joining together gives us the power to make a difference in our condition. "Can" implies both our will to act, our capacity, and the assumption that objective reality, the "cold" stream, may bend to our will.

No wonder Barack Obama evoked "Si se puede" for his outsider-style electoral campaign in 2008. When he borrowed "Yes we can" from the United Farmworkers Union, he clearly understood the slogan's importance for attracting Hispanic votes, but he was also capitalizing on the social-movement nature of the slogan, and its tie to his own writing about hope.[21] Could a black man really be elected as president of the United States only one generation after the establishment of legal equality between blacks and whites? In the speech in which Obama laid out his campaign slogan, most of his references were to other such movements, including the Founding Fathers, slaves and abolitionists, workers organizing trade unions, women seeking the vote, and the civil rights movement. "Yes we can" implied active, ongoing collective energy mobilized for common goals, even if that energy, evoked by the election campaign, was then left to wither after Obama won and began to govern.

Electing the first African American president was a major historical breakthrough, and it could not have happened without significant grassroots mobilization. It was bound to foster disillusionment, given the otherwise top-down and money-dominated nature of American politics and Obama's own within-the-system moderation. But Obama's turn to "Yes we can" and "hope" tells us a great deal. First, as he made clear again and again, his very appearance on the scene had been made possible by the civil rights movement. Second, however controversial it was in the 1960s, it and America's other great movements were central to the country's moral and political outlook. Each of the specific movements, as well as the election of an African American president, drew from and contributed to a wider climate of social hope.

The Wider Climate

That wider climate becomes essential to a movement. It consists of both an accumulation of the results of previous struggles and an expanding and deepening consensus on social morality those results have created—the sorts of treatment that humans are entitled to expect from other humans. I have said that such goals inevitably become posed in moral terms. A sense of right and wrong and, more and more, an appeal to human rights are essential aspects of a movement's motivation and public face. In labor conflicts, for example, it may involve asserting that workers have a *right* to a living wage, to form unions, to have a voice in the conditions of their work, or to control the conditions of their representation. This has included, and might one day again include, a right to the product of their labor or even to control of the means of production.

The civil rights movement's moral appeal was both religious and secular. Martin Luther King, Jr.'s first political speech, after the first day of the Montgomery bus boycott, intoned that "we are tired" of the oppression and humiliation to which African Americans had been subjected, and then went on to invoke the highest moral authorities possible:

> And we are not wrong; we are not wrong in what we are doing. If we are wrong, the Supreme Court of this nation is wrong. If we are wrong, the Constitution of the United States is wrong. If we are wrong, God Almighty is wrong. If we are wrong, Je-

sus of Nazareth was merely a utopian dreamer that never came down to earth. If we are wrong, justice is a lie, love has no meaning. And we are determined here in Montgomery to work and fight until justice runs down like water and righteousness like a mighty stream.[22]

Ministers played an essential role, no doubt because of their place in African American communities and the organizational resources over which they disposed. But they were also the appropriate people to voice the moral appeals that were especially necessary for a minority movement in that place and time. Thus the lasting importance to the movement of the Southern Christian Leadership Conference, which remained central long after the roles of SNCC and CORE had come and gone.

Appeal to a wider moral climate is always essential. This is one reason why other movements, such as Solidarity in Poland, built themselves around religious institutions. And even where other forces were more important, as in South Africa and in the drive to organize automobile workers, leadership roles were played by ministers such as Desmond Tutu in the one case and Homer Martin in the other.

Other movements have drawn from the organized left for resources, leadership, vision, moral justification and connection to wider struggles. As Golin says, "The IWW organizers brought democratic and nonviolent techniques of organization, innovative ways of actively involving women and immigrants, and a vision of America as the place where the working class of the world could come together." In addition, many of the silk workers were socialists, and their party gave them publicity and financial support. And then, in the "moment of 1913," intellectuals and artists in New York's Greenwich Village, loosely organized, became drawn to the strikers, gave them support, and helped create the Pageant in which they presented their cause to New York workers.

I have mentioned that in the UAW, communist and socialist activists among the strikers played a key role, bringing organizational skills and resources to other auto workers. Just as important, they contributed their sense of mission and connection with a larger climate of values, and a historical vision of the ultimate victory of the working class and its place in universal moral and social progress. This was also the case in South Africa, as the large and well organized Communist Party played a key role in the struggle to end apartheid, including creation of an internal underground organization capable of withstanding and combating the South African police state, and Umkhonto We Sizwe, the guerrilla army that trained abroad and infiltrated back into South Africa to carry out the "armed struggle." The Communist Party's resources, and especially its connection with external forces, were essential to keeping the movement going to end apartheid, but so was the vision it conveyed of a future nonracial socialist society.

Human Rights

Social movements feel and proclaim the justice of their cause, and explain themselves in terms of universal principles of social morality. Forging themselves in often sharp struggle against dominant structures, attitudes, and norms, each one must find ways to justify itself to itself and its antagonists, and simultaneously appeal for support to a wider community. Today the best expression of this process is in the United Nations Universal Declaration of Human Rights and its subsequent covenants.

Beginning by proclaiming that "recognition of the inherent dignity and of the equal and inalienable rights of all members of the human family is the foundation of freedom, justice and peace in the world," the declaration stresses civil and political rights including the prohibition of slavery and torture, and the right to citizenship, property, equal protection under the law, democratic participation in government, and freedom of religion. Since the declaration was proclaimed in 1948, people all over the world have further spelled out what it means to be human—in thinking, writing, and teaching; in response to new technical, political, and cultural possibilities; and, most sharply and dramatically, in political struggles.

Many who at first were voiceless, especially colonial peoples in Africa and Asia, demanded to be included, which explains in part why the Universal Declaration of Han Rights was followed in 1966 by international covenants on civil and political rights and on economic, social, and cultural rights. Both of these documents stress that "the ideal of free human beings enjoying freedom from fear and want can only be achieved if conditions are created whereby everyone may enjoy his economic, social, and cultural rights, as well as his civil and political rights."

Obviously these are still only promises, broken as often as honored. But they have become an important dimension of what hope is today by calling for higher education that is "equally accessible to all," the right to work, the right to "the highest standard of physical and mental health," the right to an adequate standard of living, and equal rights for women and equal pay for equal work. There is good reason to be cynical about these wish lists, promises made in 1948 and 1966 by governments that in many cases were colonialist, racist, and despotic. Many governments were managing inequalities that they had no intention of dismantling.

But rather than dismissing these espoused rights as empty rhetoric, it is more correct to place the ideas historically. These hopes could never have been put on a collective agenda of humanity three hundred, two hundred, or even a hundred years earlier. Universal rights began to be formulated during the Enlightenment, long before there was any collective institution to speak for humanity, and they were added to by the various democratic movements of the next two centuries. Indeed, such a declaration would have been impossible before the racialized cataclysm of World War II. For instance, several of the concepts of "universal brotherhood" embodied in the declaration were unthinkable even in liberal societies of the 1920s and 1930s, thanks to racialized concepts of biology, which only became become politically discredited after the war.

By the middle of the twentieth century, particular countries, the Catholic Church, and political and social movements almost everywhere had evolved to a point where such ideas of human rights were becoming not only widespread but also politically compelling. Historical change had put on the agenda of humankind "the advent of a world in which human beings shall enjoy freedom of speech and belief and freedom from fear and want." Despite enormous resistance, rulers and ruled together now accepted the demands contained in the declaration and the covenants as the norms by which they would agree to have their societies be judged. Generated by movements of the past and present, they can be appealed to by future movements that can find in them sources of validation and encouragement to struggle.

Hope and the Wider World

The existence of these norms highlights an essential fact about every modern movement for progressive social change: they cannot achieve their goals by themselves. No movement is ever large enough, strong enough, or united enough to win without help from outside its ranks. I have mentioned that this understanding was built into the civil rights movement, which was based in 10 percent of the American population and which sought equality in a region of the country dominated by a racist establishment in total control of the economy, politics, law enforcement, and the media. The African American minority may have been inspired by the winding down of colonialism in black Africa, but being no more than a minority, their situation at home was a radically different one. Thus civil rights strategy had to be directed as much at gaining the support of the majority, as embodied in the Supreme Court, the federal government, and Northern white opinion, as it was at mobilizing against racist practices and laws locally. This generated tensions within the movement, or rather, the civil rights movement necessarily became many movements prioritizing different targets, developing different strategies, and often disagreeing with each other over the extent and kinds of dependence on nonmovement forces.

This in gaining the support not merely of nonparticipants most likely to support the cause but also of a much broader community that in the end may decide the issue. In the case of the UAW's 1937 sit-down strike in Flint, despite the fact that General Motors devoted enormous efforts to shaping public opinion, and despite a hostile pro-GM Flint establishment and GM's immense publicity resources, the UAW won the argument with the wider public. At least it won sufficiently so that key elected officials—Governor Murphy and President Roosevelt—ended up playing crucial roles. Both men took the rare position of not favoring the employer, and of insisting that negotiations took place on a level playing field. Murphy allowed the strikers to get state relief, kept the heat and lights on at the occupied plants, used the National Guard to keep the peace rather than to break the sit-down or enforce injunctions, and actively presided over negotiations.

Beginning in the 1950s, the African National Congress turned to that moral climate, evoking it to explain and justify its nonracial movement. Of course it also sought outside material support for that struggle, eventually receiving it in various important ways from countries including the Soviet Union and Eastern Europe, Cuba, Scandinavia, and the European Union, as well as supportive movements in Britain and the United States. But it also sought moral support by bringing South Africa's apartheid system before the United Nations. In doing so, the ANC appealed to the rights, flouted by South Africa's government, that were codified in the Universal Declaration of Human Rights.

The ANC had voiced its aspirations by adopting the Freedom Charter at a mass meeting in June 1955 that was attended by 2,222 Africans, 320 Indians, 230 coloreds, and 112 whites. In its preamble and main points, the charter reflected the long arc of the history, theory, and practice of freedom outside South Africa, arguing that "no government can justly claim authority unless it is based on the will of all the people; that our people have been robbed of their birthright to land, liberty and peace by a form of government founded on injustice and inequality; that our country will never be prosperous or free until all our people live in brotherhood, enjoying equal rights and opportunities; that only a democratic state, based on the will of all the people, can secure to all their birthright without distinction of colour, race, sex or belief. . . ." Here, as throughout the entire document, we hear echoes of other histories, as well as the new precision given to "all our people": rejecting discrimination by "colour, race, sex or belief."

It is important to see this as more than rhetorical boilerplate because, as in the American civil rights movement, the sense of being in the right was an essential source of hope. Black South Africans came to conclude, in a way that helped shape their own identity and sustained them in struggle, that it was unthinkable in a world whose watchwords had become human rights, democracy, and socialism that they should have to submit forever to weird, clearly regressive, and brutal forms of domination—especially in a country in which they were the vast majority.

When History Smiles on Us

All struggles, like it or not, come to depend on the wider world, whether that be for sympathetic help from outside, for the intervention of nonparticipants, or for the effects of an encouraging moral climate. This is no less true when a revolutionary movement is able to take full power. Even the Bolsheviks, who scandalized more moderate socialists by daring to seize power at the head of Russia's radical workers, were painfully aware of representing at best a minority of the country. They were able to take power virtually without violence in Petrograd, where they had been winning over the politically active majority while the provisional government was losing their support. Rulers of a mostly peasant society, facing Russia's legendary backwardness, they looked at first eagerly and then forlornly to German revolutionaries to save them from what would become catastrophic isolation. Isaac Deutscher appropriately characterized the dismal situation in which the Bolsheviks found themselves three years later after winning the civil war and vanquishing all other opposition: defeat in victory.[23]

History had seemed to smile on the Bolsheviks, but as it turned out, that was only during the run-up to the October Revolution and shortly after. Their capacities and social power, as well as their place in the wider world, turned out to be profoundly limited. Reality confounded their hopes. Which is not to say that their hopes were foolish, but only that the failure of the German revolution left them marooned. The stage was set for the disasters to come.

The point is that social hope can never overcome its dependence on events and forces beyond control; that is of its essence. Yes, realistically calculating the balance of forces is necessary, as is calculating our own capacities and energies, but these will always include the wider world. If history does indeed smile on us, we may accomplish what we set out to do. But if not, defeat beckons.

A movement's defeat is bad enough, but South Africans and African Americans experienced this again and again and did not lose hope. Given the actual balance of forces and the nature of their struggle, they knew that there was no single correct strategy that might rescue them from losing battle after battle.[24] Far worse than defeats, movements are susceptible to an illusory way of thinking that can destroy them: We would have won if only we had gotten it right. If only we had tried harder, if only we had followed the right strategy, if only we had found the right combination of analysis and organization, if only. . . . In other words, there is a false assumption that our own efforts alone determine failure or success. But this attitude can lead to destroying the movement itself. This is what happens when the *we*, unable or unwilling to accept defeat, turns on itself, loses its sense of common purpose, and disintegrates. In Paterson, after the strike ended with the decision by some of the unions and their members to return to work, this happened within the IWW and among the Greenwich Village intellectuals most involved in creating the Pageant. Neither recovered from the fallout of the defeat, and defeat became disaster.

This chapter's final note, then, must be about the fragility of social hope—which depends so much on events and forces beyond control. Fragility is part and parcel of this strange entity, the *we* that brings us to hope and hope to us. A thousand things can diminish our will, our awareness of our capacities, our belief in being right, our sense of power, and our sense of connection to larger social forces and being part of history's moral arc. Despite all efforts to institutionalize all of this in parties and organizations, something will always escape our calculations, and social hope will always be a gamble. This hope is, in the final analysis, no more and no less than the living sense of purpose shared by real people acting together.

Chapter 3
Progress versus Hope

The kind of hope I have been talking about is not an attitude or a mood or, least of all, a feeling. It is rather a stance, a disposition to act, and to do so not individually but collectively. Yet no sooner do we begin to form a sense of its features and recognize its distinctive presence in the modern world than we become diverted. We have become caught up in, and now many of us are disillusioned by, a false hope by the name of Progress. Progress confuses us with its puzzling mixture of truth and delusion, its expectant passivity, its secularized faith. Progress is the lie of hope, yet it has been so real, so palpable in every direction that it has appeared irrefutable. In fact, hope and Progress are modernity's twin siblings, whose histories are entwined, and which often seem indistinguishable. Yet in fact modern hope and Progress, ostensibly born at the same time and so similar, have become not only opposites, but antagonists.

We have seen the hopes of movements arise, expand, and travel, following their complex, human-centered and human-created logics, even moving from place to place and time to time. In the United States slavery has been abolished, women have won the right to vote, segregation has become illegal, women have achieved greater and greater equality with men, and gays and lesbians have made themselves visible and demanded the same rights as anyone else, including same-sex marriage, which has lately advanced by sudden leaps. Human actions have made specific oppressions unacceptable, immoral, illegal, obsolete. Yes, this is an undeniable progress—against all skepticism a lower-case progress in how people treat each other, in human social morality. Not some sort of force moving on its own, improvement in social morality has been propelled by the kinds of activist social hope I have been talking about. Yet even as it leads to much human progress, social hope can be confused with, but is radically different from, this force called Progress. I capitalize Progress, as has often been done by certain proponents, to indicate some quasinatural force operating independently of human will and cumulatively making human life better. Belief in this Progress has come to counsel acceptance of or submission to social processes that seemingly operate on their own but in fact serve the dominant interests that are their sponsors. Its advocates have been telling us that human life is getting better due to scientific, technical, productive, political, and social changes under the rubric of Progress, and that there is no alternative to letting this Progress run our lives and our societies.

Despite countless specific improvements since the 1970s, championing Progress has more and more become the province of zealots, boosters, and diehards. Zealots: neoliberal economists and other true believers who see an "invisible hand" that magically produces cumulative beneficial results from un-controlled, separate, and even antagonistic individual human actions. Boosters: futurists who ignore the mounting impor-tance of negative trends, and who still believe in the univer-sally redeeming power of science. Diehards: those, especially politicians, who are professionally or ideologically committed to espousing Progress or are otherwise incapable of admit-ting that things may actually be getting worse in decisive ways rather than better.[1]

Among young people, belief in Progress with a capital *P*, which once bolstered social hope and its activists, now seems to have declined drastically. There are many reasons for this, including the cynicism I will explore in the next chapter, but surely among these reasons are the economic and technologi-cal whirlwinds that have been buffeting us about for the last generation. Endless change has become the very stuff of our daily existence, imposing constant disruption and new pos-sibilities and threats, as well as novelty and obsolescence, ev-erywhere we turn. It affects the prospects for young and old, directing where and how and whether people work, what we see and do, whom and how we know, the built and natural landscape, and our very thoughts and feelings. This Progress, out of control, constantly churning up everything, allegedly bringing "creative destruction," has been multiplying problems and offering few solutions. Above all, the human and natural ecologies are being upset by our world's ultimate engine of Progress—economic growth in pursuit of profit. The earth, our own lives, and even the protected spaces where we might seek escape are increasingly transformed by purposefully uncon-trolled commodification, innovation, calculation, marketing, and exploitation. It is a maelstrom from which nothing and no place appears exempt.

Even the most alarming result of Progress, global warming, is met with denial and paralysis. The damage of climate change may be limited, if at all, only by bringing economic growth under social control. But the most distinctive, even celebrated feature of the current global capitalist economy is precisely that it is out of anyone's control.

Small wonder there has been a disillusioned mood among intellectuals toward Progress, and a loss of its theoretical credence. Even so, advanced societies remain chained to the disruptive force of material, scientific, and technological change driven by the vicissitudes of capitalism. Progress is becoming the great enemy of humankind. Hope, today and in the future, will have to take shape in opposition to this Progress.

Ideas of Hope and Progress

In describing what hope is, the last chapter attempted to correct the conceptual error of fetishizing it as some sort of thing to be gained or lost, an entity that some people have and others lack. Hope is better understood as a key dimension of an active, collective stance, and can be read off from the process of humans changing their social reality. Even more confusing is the treatment of progress as an autonomous force that is often written with a capital *P*. More than a conceptual error, talk about Progress as an objective force, independent of human will and activity, is a political error. This reification pretends that social processes operate on their own, separate from human purposes, structures, and institutions, including relations of power. It may well be true that Progress happens to humans, imposes itself on us—but to accept that it is built into reality as such is to counsel submission.

As this takes place in the history of ideas, two things happen. One of these things is that hope understandably becomes connected with the various strands of technological, economic, social, and political change drawn together under the idea of progress. The other is that these strands become fetishized into a grand narrative, Progress with a capital *P*, which becomes treated as a law of history sometimes encouraging hopeful collective action (Victory is inevitable) but at other times, and increasingly, advising passivity and submission (Defeat is inevitable). Hope for the future, increasingly attached to Progress, by today has become suffocated by it.

Accordingly, we must now disentangle hope from Progress. Among the Greeks, hope was not taken as a simple good, as in the mythical story of Pandora's box. Pandora defied Zeus's command and opened the jar containing all the evils that might plague humans, letting them loose on the world. When she managed to close the jar, only hope, its last occupant, remained trapped inside. Greek and Roman philosophers thought about hope but were ambivalent about it, keenly aware as they were of the degeneration and ultimate death of every living thing. While, according to Sophocles, "it is hope that is the sustenance of most mortals,"[2] Epicurus and Lucretius, as well as the Stoics—given their projects of minimizing needs and desires as the only possible path to tranquility—warned against the dangers of a hopeful disposition.

But in Christianity, hope becomes an essential theme. Of course, as St. Thomas Aquinas said, it is a "theological virtue" that, whatever its applicability to daily life, ultimately has

God for its object, pointing not toward earthly well-being but to eternal life.[3] The great paradox of the hope underpinning Christianity for most of its history lies in its anticipation of the eternal beatitude of union with God. Pointing toward perfect happiness in the next life, the medieval Christian church was an organized structure of hope in a world of subjection and poverty. With all its institutions and officials, outlooks and practices, Christianity's boundless hope is built on the denigration of life itself, making this greatest of human hopes inseparable from the most profound renunciation.

Toward the beginning of the modern period, otherworldly hopes, still aiming at Christian salvation, began to combine with collective, militant, and secular movements. The Reformation incited the Peasant Wars, millenarian sects, and projects of creating God's kingdom on earth that spread from the Hutterites in Germany to Calvin's Geneva to the Massachusetts Bay. Seeking to anticipate God's kingdom of heaven in this life, such movements brought the most intense of Christian hopes down to earth.

With the Enlightenment, the French and American Revolutions, and the industrial revolution, the otherworldliness of hope continued to fade. The hope described in the previous chapter, experienced and acted on collectively—the widespread social hope for a good life for humans on earth, to be brought about by our activity—is the child of modernity. Modernity was synonymous with shifting focus away from the heavens and the afterlife and absorbing ourselves in the human, the terrestrial future, and the here and now. This is epitomized in Condorcet's *Sketch for a Historical Picture of the Progress of the Human Mind*, written while he was in hiding from the Terror, which would end his life in 1794. Condorcet concludes with a stirring vision of the future based on the cumulative advance of science, human rationality, and equality, and implying the steady decline of superstition and religion.

> Our hopes for the future condition of the human race can be subsumed under three important heads: the abolition of inequality between nations, the progress of equality within each nation, and the true perfection of mankind. Will all nations one day attain that state of civilization which the most enlightened, the freest and the least burdened by prejudices, such as the French and the Anglo-Americans, have attained already? Will the vast gulf that separates these peoples from the slavery of nations under the rule of monarchs, from the barbarism of African tribes, from the ignorance of savages, little by little disappear?[4]
>
> [...]
>
> The time will therefore come when the sun will shine only on free men who know no other master but their reason; when tyrants and slaves, priests and their stupid or hypocritical instruments will exist only in works of history and on the stage; and when we shall think of them only to pity their victims and their dupes; to maintain ourselves in a state of vigilance by thinking on their excesses; and to learn how to recognize and so to destroy, by force of reason, the first seeds of tyranny and superstition, should they ever dare to reappear amongst us.[5]

This then is the Enlightenment vision of progress as it enters the nineteenth century: human life, which has improved over time, will continue to improve in an interconnected and cumulative process building upon the spread of rationality, the growth of science and technology, and the deepening of knowledge, as well as increasing freedom and equality. At the same time, according to Condorcet, progress entails Europe and America's civilizing mission toward the rest of the world—which, he explicitly notes, implies conquest and perhaps even genocide.[6]

Progress with a Capital P

How did progress become Progress? During the nineteenth century, thinking about progress developed in two contrary directions. It is in Auguste Comte that we see the self-conscious transformation of the complex and many-sided notion of progress into Progress: a full-fledged law of history (with Spencer it becomes indeed a law of nature) raised above humans, excluding significant social and political change. Comte stresses "order," rejects equality and popular sovereignty, and emphasizes above all scientific-technological development led by a new elite. Condorcet's earlier hopeful vision of social *and* political *and* scientific *and* technological *and* economic amelioration, all joined to each other, leading to a flowering of human development led by Europe and America, is repressed. Indeed, Comte, writing thirty years after Condorcet, is terrified of what I am calling *social* progress. Combating "anarchy," his project is to provide the intellectual basis for the new "positive" state of society. Visions of individual flowering are abandoned in favor of a hierarchical society whose main goal is to produce as efficiently as possible. Comte claims to seek the definitive installation of a new order, but by attacking the subversive trends of social progress in favor of *more*—more development within the existing order.[7]

Now a full-fledged ideology, Progress came to increasingly

place the burden of change on science and technology within prevailing relations of production and social and political structures. Viewing and being acted upon by these impersonal forces, humans were seen more and more as spectators of their history rather than as participants. Progress became a kind of fetish of the future, celebrating the sheer accumulation of new discoveries and techniques.[8] The resulting grand narrative told and exaggerated a part of the story, removed dissenting and democratizing politics from the equation, and served the ruling interests and their projects of controlled transformation.

This Progress was a major theme of the great nineteenth-century world's fairs that began with London's Crystal Palace in 1851 and included commemorations of American independence (Philadelphia, 1876), the French Revolution (Paris, 1889), and Columbus's landing (Chicago, 1893). Each of these fairs featured thousands of displays showing the latest achievements in science, industry, transportation, agriculture, architecture (including the Eiffel Tower), and the arts.[9] During its six months' run, in a country of less than seventy million people, twenty-seven million people attended the Columbian Exposition. Seven years later, the turn of the twentieth century was accompanied by a widespread sense of anticipation and celebration.[10] Looking ahead to humanity's collective future shaped by new inventions, techniques, and products was now an essential aspect of the outlook of the most advanced societies.

Marxism: Recovering Hope from Progress

That was the semiofficial notion of Progress to which industrializing societies have been devoted ever since. Rejecting this word as a key ideological prop of the economic and social system they opposed, Marx and Engels present a very different notion of progress in their unforgettable paean to material progress under capitalism, the most stirring description of capitalism ever written. It concludes with the famous lines:

> The bourgeoisie, during its rule of scarce one hundred years, has created more massive and more colossal productive forces than have all preceding generations together. Subjection of Nature's forces to man, machinery, application of chemistry to industry and agriculture, steam-navigation, railways, electric telegraphs, clearing of whole continents for cultivation, canalization of rivers, whole populations conjured out of the ground—what earlier century had even a presentiment that such productive forces slumbered in the lap of social labor?[11]

They continue by describing the other side of the story. Capitalism's periodic economic crises make it like "the sorcerer who is no longer able to control the powers of the nether world whom he has called up by his spells." And, equally fatal, capitalism depends on and brings into being the "modern laborer" who, "instead of rising with the process of industry, sinks deeper and deeper below the conditions of existence of his own class. He becomes a pauper, and pauperism develops more rapidly than population and wealth." Because "society can no longer live under this bourgeoisie," Marx and Engels anticipate that the working class will unite, struggle against it, and eventually will overthrow it. Then the scientific, technical, and productive achievements instigated by the bourgeoisie in its pursuit of profit will be liberated to be used for the common good.

In this dialectical vision, technical and economic progress

is simultaneously beneficial and destructive: transforming the world, but doing so primarily for the benefit of the owners of capital, creating poverty alongside wealth, constant chaos as well as the prospect, and only the prospect, of universal freedom and well-being. This can be achieved only if and when a movement of the working class overthrows the bourgeoisie and places itself in power. When Marx and Engels avoided using the term "progress" despite their enthusiasm for the industrial revolution, their reticence reflected the skepticism emerging among those who would champion social progress making use of industrial progress. Those who supported this progress, rooted in popular struggles of the kind described in the previous chapter, were fiercely opposed to those who foresaw further economic and technical development that would be confined within a stabilized capitalist order.

Marxism bases itself firmly on the objective achievements of the bourgeoisie in harnessing knowledge, techniques, and tools bequeathed by the past as it "creates a world after its own image." In describing the operations of capitalism leading to its demise, Marx describes "tendencies working with iron necessity towards inevitable results." Nevertheless, the emancipation of the working class must come from "the workers themselves." This many-sided approach can sometimes encourage an active, participatory social hope, but it sometimes lends its participants a sense of inevitability that can be alternately consoling and demobilizing.

Non-Marxist Social Hope

Of course Marxism was not the only way of conceptualizing and pursuing social hope; it was only the most coherent and organized way. Before, during, and after Marxism there have been countless other movements—sometimes local, usually more limited, often theoretically less sophisticated—that actively demand fulfillment and extension of Enlightenment promises while refusing to wait on objective currents of history.

Martin Luther King's "Letter from Birmingham Jail" expresses the refusal to wait on larger processes, and the determination to make change happen. King asks the white moderates who criticize direct action to "reject the myth concerning time in relation to the struggle for freedom"—the notion that time itself will bring about improvements. It is a "tragic misconception of time"—indeed, a "strangely irrational notion that there is something in the very flow of time that will inevitably cure all ills." In rejecting any sense of inevitable Progress, King insists on moving from the passive mode to an active one:

> Human progress never rolls in on wheels of inevitability; it comes through the tireless efforts of men willing to be co-workers with God, and without this hard work, time itself becomes an ally of the forces of social stagnation. We must use time creatively, in the knowledge that the time is always ripe to do right. Now is the time to make real the promise of democracy and transform our pending national elegy into a creative psalm of brotherhood. Now is the time to lift our national policy from the quicksand of racial injustice to the solid rock of human dignity.[12]

While King counted on God's blessing, the civil rights movement did not wait on God. Rather, it insisted that social progress was not brought about by an impersonal force imposing itself on individuals. Rather, its every step entailed collective decisions and actions—to boycott Montgomery's bus system, for example, or to sit in at lunch counters, to break the color barrier on interstate buses and at waiting rooms, to demonstrate against police brutality, to register voters, to run election campaigns outside the segregated political system, to appeal to Northern white churches for support, or to demand federal intervention and legislation. In the process, African Americans who had been defined by segregation as humans who were less than human acted as fully human by demanding their rights. Facing intimidation, beatings, jail, firebombings, and murder, they kept on until, with the very reluctant aid of the federal government, they began to change the system and their place in it.

Realities of Progress: Living Better

When, at the outset of this chapter, I called Progress the lie of hope, I was talking not about this kind of social progress, but about the daily life progress that is so real and palpable, as in the current revolution in communication which changes our world before our eyes. The progress we constantly experience has been making life sometimes better and sometimes worse. But how can progress be both an irrefutable part of life and a lie?

The "positive megatrends" that have been making human life better include a rising infant survival rate; a rising average life span; a rising standard of living; an increasing general quality of living worldwide; increased gross product; the explosion of knowledge and knowhow; increases in food production; wider distribution of energy; the discovery, transformation, and use of raw materials; worldwide distribution of manufactured goods; world trade; world travel; literacy; tele-connectivity; computational power; and a growing ecological consciousness.[13] Despite the skepticism of postmodernists and the sharp attacks of critics like John Gray,[14] recent advocates of progress like Matt Ridley and Charles Kenney[15] point to how far we have come from daily life in premodern times. In the words of Steven Pinker:

> Our ancestors, they remind us, were infested with lice and para-sites and lived above cellars heaped with their own faeces. Food was bland, monotonous and intermittent. Health care consisted of the doctor's saw and the dentist's pliers. Both sexes labored from sunrise to sundown, whereupon they were plunged into darkness. Winter meant months of hunger, boredom, and gnaw-ing loneliness in snowbound farmhouses.
>
> But it was not just mundane physical comforts that our re-cent ancestors did without. It was also the higher and nobler things in life, beauty and human connection. Until recently most people never traveled more than a few miles from their place of birth. Everyone was ignorant of the vastness of the cosmos, the prehistory of civilization, the genealogy of living things, the ge-netic code, the microscopic world, and the constituents of matter and life. Musical recordings, affordable books, instant News of the world, reproductions of great art, and filmed dramas were inconceivable, let alone available in a tool that can fit in a shirt pocket. When children emigrated, their parents might never see them again, or hear their voices, or meet their grandchildren. And then there are modernity's gifts of life itself: the additional decades of existence, the mothers who live to see their newborns, the children who survive their first years on earth. . . .[16]

Explicitly combating antiprogress nostalgia, Pinker eloquently documents what "may be the most significant and least appreciated development in the history of our species"—that violence has declined over time, most notably in the past century. This massive historical shift is due in part to the increased intelligence of individuals shaped by the "forces of modernity—reason, science, humanism, individual rights."[17]

Living Better or Living Worse?

If things are so good, why do they feel so bad? Despite all of our once fabulous but now mundane powers, comforts, and well-being, who today besides a Steven Pinker or a Matt Ridley has the positive anticipation of the generations stirred by Condorcet or Marx? At the beginning of the twentieth century the word "progress," capitalized or not, was on the lips of many: those passionate about new technologies, partisans of capitalist industrialism, advocates of the "white man's burden" of "civilizing" foreign natives, socialists who foresaw more rational and equal forms of society, workers who attended evening classes, reformers who called themselves "Progressives," believers in the spread of democracy, secularists anticipating the demise of religious "superstition," and all the newspaper readers who were told at New Year's 1901 that in the new century they would "live longer, and be taller, healthier and more beautiful in every way."[18]

A century later, Y2K felt rather different. Although consumer society could not put off commemorations of the millennium until its actual start, so that they instead took place a year early on January 1, 2000, they were marked by nightmarish fears of computer breakdowns as well as technically brilliant shows televised around the world, and were accompanied by little hope that a better life was coming. Despite truly wondrous improvements in technology, the broad and deep Enlightenment optimism about the future has largely vanished—except among boosters, zealots, and politicians. To be sure, the global consumer society has trained us to anticipate the "next big thing." However, we have lost Condorcet's expectation of continuing progress in enlightenment, equality, and freedom, not to mention Marx's vision of a society "in which the free development of each is the condition for the free development of all."[19] And while nothing rules out further breakthroughs in medicine, science, technology, or culture that may still have vast positive effects, we no longer look forward to the promise of any of this creating universal prosperity, or creating an enlightened population, or increasing democracy—or even reducing work hours, generating more secure employment, creating greater equality, increasing social mobility, or making old age more secure.

There has been a clear change of mood since the mid-1970s. Despite vast numbers of specific improvements that everyone uses, it has slowly been dawning that life is not getting better, societies are not improving, and crises are multiplying with no solutions in sight. The planet is overheating, and the "crisis of confidence" famously described by Jimmy Carter in 1979 (and then understandably denied by every subsequent president) has only worsened.

Causes

Progress has lost its ability to inspire us. Why? Remarkably enough, it has not been because of the disasters that are a

result of progress, caused by the immense destructiveness un-
leashed during the last century, when one hundred million
people died in foreign and civil wars, genocide, and revolutionary upheavals. Hitler and Stalin, the two world wars, and Hiro-
shima and Nagasaki certainly disillusioned many people about
the world's direction. But remarkably, the period from 1933 to
1945 was not fatal to the belief in progress.[20] Writing in the
midst of what later came to be called "Les Trentes Glorieuses,"
the golden years between 1945 and 1975, Sidney Pollard put his
finger on some of the key reasons for both denial and enthusiasm in the advanced industrial societies: "material prosperity,
technical innovation and social peace."[21] The "social peace"
was expressed in labor and social-democratic participation in
governments and in formulations of social policy, including
the expansion of welfare states and capital-labor cooperation
that gave workers hitherto unimagined shares of the rising
productivity and profits. On the left, socialist and labor parties
gained confidence and a sense of direction from this truce with
capitalism. Further to the left, the Soviet victory over Nazism
even lent credence to Stalin's policy of "breaking eggs" to make
an omelet—that is, the idea that Soviet development might
one day show even Stalin's brutality to have been a factor of
historical progress.[22]

Google Ngrams show the late 1960s to be the peak years
for uses of the term "progress" in Spanish, Italian, French, and
German books. Mentions rose steeply during the 1940s, and
after reaching their peak in the 1960s, they have been in a no
less steep decline ever since. A similar decline, though not the
same pattern of increase, is true for mentions of "progress"
in English. What has happened since the 1960s to diminish
the belief in progress? To put it most simply, the conditions

nurturing faith in progress—especially economic growth, social peace, and confidence in the future of socialism and even communism—were overtaken by events. Social peace unwound during the 1960s, material prosperity declined shortly after, and a concern for the environment has been growing ever since.[23] The relative social peace and prosperity of the postwar years have given way to widespread deprivation, greater inequality, reduced social solidarity, and increased insecurity. "For the first time in the history of our country," Carter noted in that notorious 1979 speech, "a majority of our people believe that the next five years will be worse than the past five years."[24]

Deeper Causes

The oil shock of the 1970s introduced into the advanced societies a sharp consciousness about diminishing resources. This shaken confidence was the main theme of economist Robert Heilbroner's *The Human Prospect*, published in 1975, which began with the troubling question: "Is there hope for man?" and ended with a shrug. After describing the grave problems confronting humanity (overpopulation, dwindling resources, environmental damage) and their primary cause (economies geared to endless growth), he concluded by wondering whether humans had the capacities to face these problems.[25]

Heilbroner's doubts proved to be prescient, because the wholesale commitment to profit and economic growth has remained unchanged. Advanced societies seem to be in a "progress trap"—Ronald Wright's term pointing to societies that have historically undermined themselves to the point of self-destruction by blindly and relentlessly pursuing the very paths that once made them successful. Hunters, for example, historically became *too good* at hunting, killing off the animals on which they lived.[26] But why do societies fall into this trap? In *Collapse*, an exploration of the possibility of civilizational breakdown based on his study of past civilizations' inability to solve their fundamental problems, Jared Diamond discusses a dozen environmental trends: the destruction of natural habitat (including wetlands, forests, coral reefs); the mismanagement and destruction of wild fish stocks; the destruction of a "significant fraction of" both animal and plant wild species; the erosion of soil and damage of farmland; the using up of major energy sources; the depletion of fresh water in lakes, rivers, and underground aquifers; the using up of available sunlight energy; the pollution of air, soil, ocean, lakes, and rivers by toxic chemicals; the transfer of "alien species" of plants and animals to places where they disrupt native species and habitats; and the problems of gases escaping into the atmosphere, human overpopulation, and destructive human impact on the environment. Each of these negative effects of human progress is out of control, increasing rapidly and combining with the other factors to magnify their destructive effect.[27]

But how is it possible to challenge this dismal trend? In addition to the environmental threats that seem to be leading to possible civilizational collapse, there is a second major negative trend: the creation of a society without opposition. Herbert Marcuse described this fifty years ago in *One-Dimensional Man*, speaking of the loss of any sense of alternatives. Unlike Diamond, Marcuse is talking not about values but about the social-political system and its absence of opposition. It is the system that generates the collective incapacity to conceive of a different world and other structures, practices, *and* values.

Marcuse argues that the advanced societies' immense productive power and—already in 1964—media wizardry create an ever richer sense of possibility, but one that is strictly contained *within* the prevailing economic, social, and political system, leading to a profound mood of resignation about alternatives and an increasing inability to think negatively about the dominant way of life. The result is a kind of democratic totalitarianism that is wholly compatible with civil rights, a free press, and free elections.[28]

We must ask: If things are so bad, why do they feel so good? The dramatic changes since the 1960s—the Vietnam War, the explosion of the New Left, the end of government-sanctioned racial segregation in the United States, feminism, the end of the prosperity of the Golden Years, victory in the Cold War, and the collapse of communism—have opened out onto a post–Cold War globalized society whose most notable opposition comes from Islamist fundamentalists, and whose most massive movement is the migration of refugees into Europe. The trends confirm *One-Dimensional Man*'s basic themes of one-dimensionality and democratic totalitarianism. Today's world is without opposition, inasmuch as free-market global capitalism rules nearly everywhere. Despite violence that is often horrific, including that of Al Qaeda and ISIS, despite important emphases on localism and sustainability, and despite furious waves of local resistance such as Brexit and the Donald Trump movement, capitalist globalization reigns unchallenged by any alternative. The financial meltdown and the Great Recession of 2008–9 led to its *indignatos*, Occupy, and eventually the rise of Bernie Sanders and Jeremy Corbyn—but the world economic system rests unchanged, the culprits who caused the financial collapse have escaped prosecution, and, however bizarre it seemed, in 2009 the Tea Party sprang to life by demanding more of the same policies that had caused the crisis in the first place. Despite the Arab Spring, change in the Middle East seems frozen between Islamist fundamentalism and dictatorship. The idea that "another world is possible" is being refuted on the ground, and the lack of any sense of a successful alternative may be one element that encourages fervent religious terrorism.

Deepest Causes

Above all, we sense no alternative to the various kinds of progress in which we are enmeshed. To get clearer about this, we must go back to distinguishing lower-case progress from upper-case Progress. From improvements in medicine to movements against racist police practices, the first kind of progress indicates human activities under human control and that express collective human intentions: progress that helps our lives, and which we deliberately make happen. From the Great Recession to global warming, the second kind of Progress still stems from human activity, but it is activity that generates forces that have been deliberately placed out of control. In other words, progress and Progress indicate not just two different kinds of ideas about how the future unfolds, but two different lived realities. To the extent that these two things are confused among us and by us, it is impossible to think clearly about our hopes and possibilities.

Our confusion is among the deeper causes of our pessimism today, but it is not yet its deepest cause. As early as 1939 a former colleague of Marcuse, Walter Benjamin, put his finger on a more fundamental and even more disturbing reality.[29] He evoked Paul Klee's painting "Angelus Novelus": a storm "irresistibly" propels the angel of history "into the future to which his back is turned, while the pile of debris before him grows skyward. This storm is what we call progress."[30] The storm and chaos is irresistible, and its detritus terrifies us, who dare not look toward the future. Benjamin is describing living in a maelstrom.

Marx and Engels describe it: "Constant revolutionizing of production, uninterrupted disturbance of all social conditions, everlasting uncertainty and agitation distinguish the bourgeois epoch from all earlier ones. All fixed, fast-frozen relations, with their train of ancient and venerable prejudices and opinions, are swept away, all new-formed ones become antiquated before they can ossify. All that is solid melts into air, all that is holy is profaned, and man is at last compelled to face with sober senses his real conditions of life, and his relations with his kind."

What if "man" does not develop the "sober senses" that would see the need for human intervention to bring the maelstrom under control? What if, especially under consumer capitalism and in the "one-dimensional society," no oppositional force emerges to face and challenge the "real conditions" of people's lives? What if that force is defeated? What if it never mobilizes sufficiently, or never becomes fully oppositional, or weakens? What if we eventually form parties and movements with only minimal goals—of controlling the maelstrom's worst effects and protecting its victims, with brief success—and then are overpowered and demoralized? What if oppositions emerge in self-defeating forms, never challenging the system that is leaving them behind, but rather turning to nativism, nationalism, and racism? In short, what if Marx and Engels's description of the problem was correct, but the solution misfires?

Then the maelstrom, Benjamin's progress, would become the permanent state of the world.

It has happened. This is why I call it Progress with a capital *P*. Keys to understanding this situation are presented by André Gorz in his *Critique of Economic Reason*, and were suggested thirty years earlier, in 1958, by John Kenneth Galbraith's *The Affluent Society*. The first key is that advanced capitalism is no longer driven by human needs. Since the beginning of the consumer economy, during the golden age of 1945 to 1975, human needs have become less and less the driving economic force, while capitalism's own need to produce and market commodities has more and more replaced it. In order to generate profit and growth, capitalism has become a vast, self-sustaining need-creation machine. In other words, according to Gorz, we have reached the point where consumption is now "*in the service of production*," which in turn is in the service of profit and growth. Unlimited growth, fueled by advertising, means that the economy, which was once only a subsystem of social life with specific and necessary tasks to perform, now "swallows up all areas of social activity."[31]

Today the negative effects carry well beyond Benjamin's storm of progress. In the era of neoliberalism the maelstrom is felt everywhere, at every instant, as economic imperatives invade all spaces and the bottom line dominates all lives. No traditions, values, or institutions effectively stand against it in a world where there is virtually nothing that cannot be marketed. The 24/7 media spectacle never stops, penetrating to the farthest reaches of the globe and the deepest reaches of consciousness. Every square inch is mapped, and Google allows us to see almost every space. There is no longer any wilderness; species extinction is happening so rapidly that it can barely be tracked, and no people are exempt from the demand to adapt or die off. As both the built and the natural worlds undergo constant construction and redevelopment, it is no longer possible to keep up with the pace of technological change or the accumulation of scientific knowledge. Parents must resign themselves to raising their children to function in this world, whose purpose and meaning increasingly escape understanding. More than Benjamin could have guessed seventy-five years ago, the maelstrom is irresistible, its detritus overwhelming, and we dare not look toward the future.

Will increasing disorder prompt a broad awareness of the destructive chaos built into the economic system—and if so, what needs to be done about it? It increasingly subjects all corners of existence to its free-market totalitarianism, with breathtaking technological progress driven by an uncontrolled push for profit that sweeps everything in its path. Although Marxism as a movement is over, its analysis remains a key to grasping this dynamic of capitalism, the ways in which the economy and its force, priorities, and logic shape the rest of our lives, right down to our attitudes and values. The capitalist economy totally depends on and feeds this constant and endless Progress in the production of goods and services. Today we are trapped in this Progress.

Although the popularity of the idea of Progress has dropped precipitously, our lived reality is one of boundless economic expansion based on free-market competition and innovation. It is today's Progress—the force deserving to be capitalized, at one and the same time placed beyond us, imposing itself on us, and, most frightening, operating within us. We never seem to develop Marx and Engels's "sober senses" about it, the awareness that we ourselves are creating and maintaining it.

They write that the society "that has conjured up such gigantic means of production and of exchange, is like the sorcerer who is no longer able to control the powers of the nether world whom he has called up by his spells."[32] Indeed.

The neoliberal project of the last generation has intensified this maelstrom, justified it, indeed blessed it, and done everything necessary to remove it from democratic social control. As Wendy Brown says, "In letting markets decide our present and future, neoliberalism wholly abandons the project of individual or collective mastery of existence."[33] Government becomes attacked as the enemy, insofar as it is the sole institution that can impose control on the increasingly "free" market. Behind an ideological appeal to the spontaneous, natural ordering of individual activity, and the Progress it must necessarily generate, stand those who benefit most from it and who have the power to make sure that their interests are dominant within it, even as the system as a whole is kept out of human control.

Of course, the appeal to progress was always part of the justification for capitalism. In April 1913, the Paterson Central Strike Committee responded to the owners' demand that each worker should henceforth operate multiple looms: "The manufacturers endeavor with specious arguments to establish the system under the guise of progress. Let us see. . . . the weaver is today asked to operate four looms instead of two, as formerly. Is this progress?"[34] The strikers were asserting their social hope by doing battle against the manufacturers' Progress, which they sought to impose as the latest necessary improvement. The workers stood for their own lower-case progress, which would give them a decisive voice in resisting the tidal force of economic "rationalization" that spelled higher profits for the owners. They lost the strike; the owners' Progress was imposed on them.

Hope against Progress

In the twenty-first century we are immersed in Progress with a capital *P*, which is no longer celebrated as the civilization's master idea as it was in the nineteenth century, but is now embraced without being named, its blind force like a law of nature acting behind our backs and asserting itself in every area of our lives. It is tempting to stop using the term "progress," with or without a capital *P*, for the various meanings that point in such different directions. Despite all our social progress and improvements in living standards and longevity, like Marx and Engels we still await agents with "sober senses" and sufficient power to bring Progress under collective human control and to master its terrifying and destructive side. Until then, the hidden rulers and beneficiaries of the maelstrom are free to urge on its blind force, to celebrate its acting behind all of our backs, and to insist that we are free and responsible for ourselves while it "naturally" continues imposing itself on every aspect of our lives.

Today, social hope depends on subverting this Progress. But it has always been the case. Writing in 1916, his reflections prompted by the First World War, John Dewey attacked the notion that rapid change, including "changes in our own comfort," meant genuine human progress. He wrote scathingly against the "childish and irresponsible"[35] faith that there is "an automatic and wholesale progress in human affairs."[36] He rejected any philosophy that "trusts the direction of human affairs to nature, or Providence, or evolution, or manifest destiny—that is to say, to accident—rather than to a contriving and constructive intelligence."[37] As he saw it, improvement "depends upon deliberate human foresight and socially constructive work."[38] Bettering life—genuine progress—depends above all on human intention and decision. Like Walter Benjamin twenty-five years later, Dewey called on his readers to do battle against a maelstrom that was beyond human control. Living today in a world wholly swept along by the storm, we are faced with a task that is even more urgent.

Chapter 4

Cynicism

As environmental dangers have intensified, as the economic system has been encouraged to invade the rest of life and grow out of control, the collective capacity for meaningful action has diminished. The causes are many, but among the foremost, spreading like cancer in the United States and the other advanced societies—multiplying molecularly without notice, yet seemingly inexorably, crowding healthy energies, devouring more and more space—is cynicism.

Like hope, cynicism covers a wide variety of attitudes and behaviors. Its cluster of meanings range from tolerance of manipulative and dishonest behavior to scorn for other people's motivations, from deeply personal disbelief in one's self and one's prospects to despair about intimate relations with others. It also embraces dismissive attitudes about localities, organizations, and institutions, encompasses resignation about human capabilities as such, or even about how nature operates. In politics, the cynic openly adopts positions in which he or she does not believe, changes views in order to get elected, or says or does whatever wins favor with political bigwigs and especially major campaign donors. Or expects others to do this, or doesn't raise an eyebrow when they do. Although people sometimes draw sweepingly negative conclusions about large political and social systems that can spur activism, fatalism is one of cynicism's more usual faces, related to but distinct from a second face, the widespread conviction that people are motivated primarily by self-interest. A third face is an acceptance of lying and manipulation as an inevitable feature of social relations. Fully developed, these attitudes degenerate into dishonesty, misanthropy, and social hopelessness, as each easily leads to the other.

It is a mood that fills the air. We experience it in the media, in the consumer culture, in politics, at work, even in personal relationships. So it is not simply something outside us, but rather a constant temptation. In the last chapter I spoke of Progress as the reification of hope, human activity converted into a thing or force drawing us along, announcing a positive future and making us into its objects and observers. The problem with cynicism is that it usually renders us passive. The enemy of hope, it assures us that our efforts are useless. Unstable and fragile, hope lives in tension with cynicism. Paradoxically, then, each is always present in the other, haunts its other. By yielding to its smug realism we free ourselves from guilt, responsibility, and the need to act, and we can devote ourselves to—ourselves. Yes, the situation is terrible, but there are so many compensations. . . .

We may consider this a bad attitude, but the cynic will find company—not often with an active sense of a collectivity, because cynicism does not usually bind people but rather separates them. But it does entail a feeling of superiority over the poor fools who simply don't grasp the way things really are, who live by illusions and wasted effort. With its devotion to "reality," cynicism has an aggressively complacent, even self-satisfied flavor. In the words of William Chaloupka's study of American cynicism today, this society is "awash in cynicism," which is "pervasive."[1] Almost every author who discusses it testifies to its recent increase: we are becoming more and more cynical, cynicism is a defining feature of American society, it is the essential attitude of the contemporary world. Peter Sloterdijk's 1980's philosophical study, *Critique of Cynical Reason*, famously put its finger on cynicism as "the dominant operating mode in contemporary culture."[2] It has come to be regarded as one of advanced society's fundamental ills, a malaise to be combated, an accusation to be levied or rebutted.[3] It is so much a cause for worry that national leaders are troubled about it, political pundits sketch proposals to neutralize it, scholars search for its roots, bipartisan commissions solemnly deliberate on how to counteract it—and politicians run against it.[4]

What Cynicism Is

In connecting the various strands of today's cynicism, political theorist Sharon Stanley nicely captures its logic: "In this corrupt world, it reasons, no one and nothing can be trusted. Everyone wears a mask beneath which naked, brutal self-interest calculates and plots. This cynicism reduces all social roles, from idealistic crusaders to cunning criminals, to this most base self-interest. The archetypal cynic cannot abide any appeal to shared values, any statement of love or virtue, without bitter incredulity and skepticism."[5]

Dictionary definitions of cynicism usually begin with the belief that people are generally selfish or dishonest. Sloterdijk goes beyond this by differentiating political leaders serving their own interest (or, we would add, the narrow interest of some of their subjects) from their political henchmen who sell their bosses' actions as something intended for the common good, and these from their subjects who reflexively reject such claims. At the top are the society's "master cynics" who publicly engage in manipulation and lies. These are assisted by supporters (including, no doubt, those who formulate and deploy their "talking points," and those who create and carry out their campaigns based on fear or resentment or nostalgia). The target of such cynical manipulation, we, the citizens and consumers, understandably respond with our own cynicism, refusing to trust what people say, further losing faith in politics and politicians and discounting the ads, although putting up with the entire spectacle.

One of the main tools of the master cynics and their agents is bullshit. Bullshit, as famously described by philosopher Harry Frankfort, is an appropriate technical term for indicating a specific mode of cynical discourse. The bullshitter is indifferent to truth or falsehood. His or her appeals have no interest in conveying information or communicating rationally, but seek only to convince. The target is masses of people, and the tools are whatever means are necessary.[6]

One result is "media cynicism." This is a blanket mistrust generated by the media's dominant focus not on understanding and evaluation of the content of political claims—though a fair amount of fact checking does take place—but rather on politics as little more than a strategic game whose goal is to convince the electorate and defeat opponents. The scorecard attitude operates, whether or not an actual contest is taking place, whenever a conversation focuses on how a politician, public figure, or corporation is *trying to appear*. In the cynical society, everyone learns that what we hear and see, irrespective of its ostensible content, is done in order to achieve this or that goal. Films like *The Candidate* and *Wag the Dog* capture this cynical view of politics. Part of the audience does indeed believe what they are told, but among those who don't, one response is to turn away from the spectacle entirely, rejecting the media as a reliable source of information. Another response is to enter a comfortable bubble in which one hears what one already believes, finding media that faithfully reflect one's own biases—Fox News, for example, where one rarely has to listen to objective analysis. Yet another response is even more deeply cynical: namely, accepting the system's pleasures and becoming complicit in its practices while no longer believing in any of it.[7]

Chaloupka finds this last theme to be the key to understanding what is common to all of today's manifestations of cynicism. "Defined concisely, cynicism is the condition of lost belief."[8] Cynics construct a way of life "against belief, or after its exhaustion."[9] Lost belief may be a broad cultural condition of secular, affluent, educated societies—no longer believing in a supreme being to reward and punish our behavior, or in objective standards of behavior, or in being able to distinguish truth from falsehood—or no longer believing in other people, in institutions, in society itself. The loss of belief in politics and government encourages a decline in voter turnout in all advanced societies.[10] And the same condition helps extreme antigovernment cynics to dominate the American and British mainstreams and succeed in selling off the public sphere and privatizing its functions. Similar attitudes, directed at public schools, say, or science, encourage other cynics to undertake home schooling, or to refuse to have their children immunized.

Sloterdijk, and Chaloupka with him, stresses ways in which lost belief can be individually and socially healthy—both promote "kynicism," which they take as an alternative that playfully and cheekily pokes fun at individuals, practices, and institutions without falling into the current negativity of cynicism. In this they evoke the playfulness of the founder of cynicism, Diogenes of Sinope, in his rejection of the by then conventional philosophy of Socrates and Plato. Stefan Lorenz Sorgner describes the outrageousness of original Greek cynicism:

> Is [it] not crude and grotesque to pick one's nose while Socrates exorcises his demon and speaks of the divine soul? Can it be called anything other than vulgar when Diogenes lets a fart fly against the Platonic theory of ideas—or is fartiness itself one of the ideas God discharged from his meditation on the genesis of the cosmos? And what is it supposed to mean when this philosophising town bum answers Plato's subtle theory of Eros by masturbating in public?[11]

Beyond cheekiness, we know that specific forms of cynicism can be stages on the way to creating movements of change, as during the anti–Vietnam War movement and during the last years of so-called socialism in the Soviet Union and Eastern Europe. Antigovernment and antisystem cynicism sometimes goes against the general trend of demoralization and leads to action rather than demobilization, and to solidarity rather than isolation. Under certain circumstances, the condition of lost belief can give rise to collective hope as new and alternative beliefs and practices become possible. This is one of the paradoxes of cynicism, which usually disempowers but at times can point people to what *must be* changed. The bitter jokes about "really existing socialism" in the Soviet Union and Eastern Europe— "Capitalism is the exploitation of man by man, and socialism is the exact opposite"; "They pretend to pay us and we pretend to work"—reflected a blanket hostility to the system that eventually drew people together to overthrow it.

Stanley writes that "cynicism is dangerous, producing a toxic form of anti-political paralysis and rendering critique impotent."[12] She thus directs us away from the broad phenomenon to the specific claim that cynicism undermines the movement-centered hope at the heart of this book. Her point is that cynicism usually dissuades people from becoming active opponents of practices, conditions, and institutions that they know are fundamentally wrong—for example, from demanding further expansion of human rights, or government regulation of the financial sector, or a living wage, or an end to free trade. But the end of communism confirms, as does this list of recent causes, that cynicism about the existing situation and its agents may point somewhere other than to a broad demoralization about change as such. Sometimes widespread cynicism may indicate that something is building that is more encouraging than the irreversible loss of hope that renders change unthinkable.

Cynicism versus Hope

Sloterdijk embraces "kynicism" in the face of a sweeping cynicism that denies the very possibility of social hope. At around the time he published his *Critique of Cynical Reason*, the slogan "There is no alternative" entered history as the watchword of a successful right-wing and authoritarian dismantling of gains won by generations of popular struggles. One major response from the left today calls itself "Podemos; We Can," and an international left battle cry against neoliberal globalization is "Another world is possible." Indeed, Sloterdijk admits that the immediate source of his book was "the pervasive sense of political disillusionment in the wake of the 1960s and the pained feeling of the lack of political and social alternatives in Western societies today."[13] The 1960s activist generation faced a time of "political disillusion, cynicism, and atrophied trust in the future" that led him to search widely and deeply for the origins and meanings of contemporary cynicism.

Revealing the underlying relations of power and interest—critiquing the society's lies, errors, and ideology—now has little effect. Today, in Sloterdijk's phrase, the dominant frame of mind is "enlightened false consciousness." This oxymoron points to the fact that people think they know the score about how the world operates, but simultaneously delude themselves. Sartre's "bad faith" is another way of characterizing the same phenomenon. The point is that people in some way know the truth about how wrong things are, yet are unable or unwilling to act on this awareness, and so wish to hide that awareness from themselves. Perhaps people do not really care anymore that millions are undernourished, that money dominates politics, that the economic and political systems are fundamentally undemocratic and starkly unequal. Slavoj Žižek, who unlike Sloterdijk still protests against this condition, sharpens the "enlightened false consciousness" formulation: in our cynicism, we continue to cover ourselves with the ideology of freedom, democracy, opportunity, and equality even while knowing that it does not depict reality.[14] If so, we live within the "capitalist realism" described by Mark Fisher, concluding that there is no alternative to our society and its practices even while no one really believes in them anymore.[15] Starting by renouncing any sense of possibility, people conclude that ours is the only reality. This is a lie, and we know it, but it eases our discomfort.

When being "realistic" is presented as his or her main claim, the cynic stresses that we live in a terrible world, but goes on to insist that this is somehow because of human nature, or the very essence of movements or institutions, and that we have no alternative to going along because change is impossible. Each step of the argument trots out as evidence some corrupt individual or practice, or some dreadful historical catastrophe, and the entire attitude mocks those who refuse to accept this reality. Compare this to social hope, as described in chapter 2 of this book. Social hope begins with the determination to take action. By seeking to discourage people from political and social activism, cynicism is not simply an argument; it is a practice. If it starts as a way of thinking about possibilities, by finding them impossible it becomes an attitude that hardens into a way of acting: inaction. In contrast, to name a group "Podemos" is a response to the widely felt opposite practice and attitude that "we can't." For many it is an irritating response, denouncing our passivity, hounding us in our comfort. Just as hope begins with a sense of possibility, cynicism attacks this with the self-fulfilling claim that nothing can be done.

Cynicism also rejects the "we" in "we can." There are indeed cynical collectivities, groups whose function is to jeer at those who come together in social hope, just as there are those on the other side who mobilize to act against them. But more relevant for us is the active inaction of those who might join movements but choose not to. This is the condition of those I described in chapter 2 as dwelling in a state of *us*ness. They exist in what

Sartre calls seriality—in passive and externally determined collectivities in which each individual acts alongside others, but in isolation from them. This prevailing experience cannot help but shape our consciousness of what might be done. If people are not disposed to act, what sense of possibility is there? Without participation with others how can a sense of *we* develop and generate a collective will to change, a sense of the group's power about being capable of doing so? By myself I inevitably have only my own consciousness and experience. This posture may not require cynicism or make it inevitable, but the experience of aloneness and separateness, busyness and selfcenteredness, the absence of active social and political participation, is the soil in which cynicism flourishes.[16]

A look at its structures refracted through the experience of social hope suggests that cynicism is more than an outlook. It does not emerge all by itself but against its opposite, with the *not* and *can't* built into it. If social hope is about people moving into a collective and active stance that redefines situations and even ourselves, it is clear why cynicism is the anti-hope. Certainly it is not always produced by isolated individuals, but is politically and socially encouraged by today's common sense: individuals cannot act collectively to solve problems. Indeed, there are scarcely any genuinely *social* problems. There is a bitterness in this stance, a hostile intelligence that mocks others as naive.[17]

Everybody Knows

In my discussion of what hope is, I cited several examples from the rich history of social hope. In contrast, it is of the essence of cynicism to produce nothing. So we can best capture its fruits in a popular song. Chaloupka titles his study of cynicism after Leonard Cohen's unforgettable lament "Everybody Knows," which begins:

> Everybody knows that the dice are loaded
> Everybody rolls with their fingers crossed
> Everybody knows that the war is over
> Everybody knows the good guys lost
> Everybody knows the fight was fixed
> The poor stay poor, the rich get rich
> That's how it goes
> Everybody knows
> Everybody knows that the boat is leaking
> Everybody knows that the captain lied
> Everybody got this broken feeling
> Like their father or their dog just died

Everybody knows. We see most political candidates win nomination by speaking the language of their base and then, without skipping a beat, moving to the center in order to appeal to the electorate at large in the general election. In the 2015 Israeli election, Benjamin Netanyahu came up with a similar scheme, unleashing rejectionist and racist appeals just before election day, winning the election, and then claiming two days later to be open to peace negotiations and promising to govern on behalf of all Israelis. The administrations of George W. Bush and Tony Blair patently lied about the presence of chemical weapons in Iraq in 2002–3, and then started a war costing tens of thousands of lives and hundreds of billions of dollars. But their crimes against humanity and against peace will never be prosecuted. The US Supreme Court based its acceptance of unlimited and undisclosed financial contributions to elections on the right of individual free speech enshrined in the US Constitution, when everybody knew that they were in fact promoting political inequality and rule of the wealthy.

The media spend much time analyzing campaign strategy as a substitute for analyzing the content of political proposals, thus turning people away from taking elections seriously as anything more than efforts to win.[18] Everybody knows that the wealthy have become more wealthy because of their ability to dominate the political process. The needs of the economic system and those who control it left human needs behind a long time ago. The system's bottom line, that reality of realities, hands out its rewards and penalties irrespective of one's contribution to the general well-being. Everybody knows, but it doesn't matter. This is today's cynicism.

Bitter and lugubrious, "Everybody Knows" is the ultimate protest song, a song about the lack of protest songs. It ends with a sense of our dangers:

> And everybody knows that the Plague is coming
> Everybody knows that it's moving fast
> Everybody knows that the naked man and woman
> Are just a shining artifact of the past
> Everybody knows the scene is dead
> But there's gonna be a meter on your bed
> That will disclose
> What everybody knows

Sources of Cynicism: Self-Interest

Earlier I mentioned several sources of cynicism: the decline of belief in Progress, the destruction of the last century, the failures of revolutions. As I've said, we live after Progress, after the Holocaust, and after Marxism. Postmodernism is even skeptical toward the Enlightenment and modernity. But our daily lives reveal at least two other sources of cynicism that are structured into our experience: we live in a society based on self-interest, and this has long since modulated into a consumer society of spectacle.

Most of the analyses bewailing cynicism today ignore the fact that in a key respect, cynicism is built into capitalism. The great economic transformation introduced by the capitalist mode of production—commodity production for the purpose of profit—was at the same time a political and social transformation, meeting society's vital needs through the market and competition. And by validating self-interest as *the* essential social principle, capitalism simultaneously involved a moral and cultural revolution. On the one hand, this meant morally legitimizing the pursuit of wealth. On the other, it proclaimed self-interest as a beneficial principle for organizing social life.

Understanding this leads us back to capitalism's two greatest theorists, Adam Smith and Karl Marx. It was, above all, Adam Smith who valued self-love, self-interest, competition, and even greed as fundamental principles.

> Man has almost constant occasion for the help of his brethren, and it is in vain for him to expect it from their benevolence only. He will be more likely to prevail if he can interest their self-love in his favour, and show them that it is for their own advantage to do for him what he requires of them. Whoever offers to another a bargain of any kind, proposes to do this. Give me that which I want, and you shall have this which you want, is the meaning of every such offer; and it is in this manner that we obtain from

one another the far greater part of those good offices which we stand in need of. It is not from the benevolence of the butcher, the brewer, or the baker that we expect our dinner, but from their regard to their own interest. We address ourselves, not to their humanity but to their self-love, and never talk to them of our own necessities but of their advantages.[19]

Self-interest works to organize society only insofar as individuals compete with each other according to the laws of supply and demand, which operate in the market as an "invisible hand" coordinating all economic activity. Thus, even though he sees self-interest as fundamental, Smith manages to avoid cynicism with his rosy description of the market and its operations as forces for the common good. Yes, he is saying, individuals are out for themselves, but not only does the market coordinate their activities; there are also other social forces that balance self-interest and the market. Smith himself, in his *Theory of Moral Sentiments*, had spelled out a moral basis for social life among self-interested individuals—the capacity for compassion and the desire to be thought well of. These restrain individuals, and the market further regulates them.[20] Furthermore, in *The Wealth of Nations* Smith gave the state dozens of functions to serve the common good even as it operates alongside the "invisible hand" of the competition-regulated market.

Smith's sense of morality and his commitment to government notwithstanding, a strong tendency to cynicism is lodged at the heart of a society that erects self-seeking and competition as its highest values. Its individuals cannot help trying to elevate themselves over others, or suspect others' claims of benevolence and generosity. *Caveat emptor*—"Let the buyer beware"—dates back to the sixteenth century, and places wariness as a core principle of all business transactions—which, as market fundamentalists insist today, are the society's most vital interactions.

That the logic of the market was not generating the common good was plain for all to see in the years between Smith and Marx. Spokesmen for the factory system. like Nassau Senior, managed to ignore the social upheaval it generated, justify child labor, excuse poverty, and not worry about the stunted generations toiling and living in inhuman conditions. Senior claimed that the wealth of the factory owner was a fitting reward for his abstinence, opposed the Poor Laws and factory legislation, and famously showed contempt for the Irish victims of the potato famine. This human cost of the factory system was compellingly shown by Marx's colleague Friedrich Engels in *The Condition of the Working Class in England in 1844*.

Marx and Engels placed the class society causing these conditions at the center of their analysis of capitalism. At its core is the relationship between capitalist and worker. Marx depicts the moment when the worker is hired, following the agreement on hours and wages. He does not deny that freedom, equality, and self-interest are essential to the society.

> This sphere . . . within whose boundaries the sale and purchase of labour-power goes on, is in fact a very Eden of the innate rights of man. There alone rule Freedom, Equality, Property and Bentham. Freedom, because both buyer and seller of a commodity, say of labour-power, are constrained only by their own free will. They contract as free agents, and the agreement they come to, is but the form in which they give legal expression to their common will. Equality, because each enters into relation

with the other, as with a simple owner of commodities, and they exchange equivalent for equivalent. Property, because each disposes only of what is his own. And Bentham, because each looks only to himself. The only force that brings them together and puts them in relation with each other, is the selfishness, the gain and the private interests of each. Each looks to himself only, and no one troubles himself about the rest, and just because they do so, do they all, in accordance with the pre-established harmony of things, or under the auspices of an all-shrewd providence, work together to their mutual advantage, for the common weal and in the interest of all.[21]

But beneath these achievements of modern society lies another relationship, one no less essential to capitalism.

On leaving this sphere of simple circulation or of exchange of commodities, which furnishes the "Free-trader Vulgaris" with his views and ideas, and with the standard by which he judges a society based on capital and wages, we think we can perceive a change in the physiognomy of our dramatis personae. He, who before was the money-owner, now strides in front as capitalist; the possessor of labour-power follows as his labourer. The one with an air of importance, smirking, intent on business; the other, timid and holding back, like one who is bringing his own hide to market and has nothing to expect but—a hiding.[22]

Marx enables us to grasp the cynicism structured into capitalism by showing the contradictions built into its essential structures and operations. Certainly his writings have a cynical tone as he talks about the bourgeoisie and their claims, and he regarded the system itself as beyond saving, but Marx the system-cynic had nothing in common with the cynicism we have been discussing, at least not in three vital respects: his regard for collective human capacities, especially of the working class; his faith in the historical process; and his devotion to describing reality free from self-interested distortion. Understanding and explaining how the system operated, and communicating it as an intellectual tool to help guide the struggles of the working class, became a major part of his life's work. This entailed exposing bourgeois ideology and the operations of capitalism, and illuminating the possible paths of proletarian struggle.

Sources of Cynicism: The Consumer Society and Its Bullshit

The experience of living under contemporary capitalism adds a distinctly new dimension of cynicism. In the most controversial section of *The Affluent Society*, Galbraith put his finger on what was new by arguing against the "myth of consumer sovereignty." As I mentioned in chapter 3, needs do not drive production, but rather are created in the process of production: the producer has the "function both of making the goods and of making the desires for them." Wants are "synthesized by advertising, catalyzed by salesmanship, and shaped by the discreet manipulations of the persuaders."[23]

In this discussion, written during the early days of the consumer society, Galbraith remarked that the wants thus created were "not very urgent" and that a higher level of production does not produce a greater degree of well-being than a lower level of production. But while these points remain no less true, the more relevant point for our understanding of today's cynicism is the process of need creation. "Increases in consumption, the counterpart of increases in production, act by suggestion or emulation to create wants. Or producers may proceed actively to create wants through advertising and salesmanship." Following but sharpening Galbraith's formulation, André Gorz pointed out that the most powerful needs driving the process belong to the capitalist system, not to its workers or its consumers.

Are people aware, even dimly, that their needs, which appear to drive the economy, are not fully their own? Do they know that in some sense they themselves are less the beneficiaries of the system of profitable production than its willing agents? Certainly they are not aware in great enough numbers to be a threat to the entire process—or, perhaps more hopefully, not yet. Perhaps they know that their needs are not fully their own, but are indifferent to that fact. Or, as Žižek and Fisher suggest, they may even like this state of affairs. The need-creating culture, amplified by the media, has become, in the formulation of Guy Debord, the society of the spectacle. This society, in which the economy totally occupies all of social life, is one "where the tangible world is replaced by a selection of images which exist above it, and which simultaneously impose themselves as the tangible *par excellence.*"[24] With "the commodity dominating all that is lived,"[25] appearances replace reality; the spectacle is everywhere and all the time. We watch it on television and on the Internet, and we live within it. It is a kind of universal consciousness, brought to us through the courtesy of our corporate advertisers.

An impressive array of cultural critics has lamented the negative effects of advertising, including Robert Heilbroner, who spoke a generation ago of its "ceaseless flow of half-truths and careful deceptions."[26] Scholars have studied "consumer cynicism" in its many forms, from resistance to marketing techniques to more systematic anticonsumerist projects. This springs from the common goal "of not being fooled by marketers."[27] But these efforts often ignore the fact that we live in a world in which public communication itself has become saturated with cynicism. Frankfort's discussion of bullshit is especially illuminating: "The realms of advertising and of public relations, and the nowadays closely related realm of politics, are replete with instances of bullshit so unmitigated that they can serve among the most indisputable and classic paradigms of the concept."[28] It is important to note that the agents of these systems are not necessarily lying, any more than they are aiming at conveying information, or facts, or the truth about situations. As Frankfort describes the bullshitter, his distinctive characteristic is that "the truth values of his statement are of no central interest to him." What he hides from us is the fact that "his intention is neither to report the truth nor to conceal it." He "is unconcerned with how the things about which he speaks truly are."[29] What then is the main concern of advertising and public relations? Having nothing to do with communicating information, with truth and falsehood, much public communication in the spectacular society is selling—seeking to persuade, to convince. The spectacular universe structures experience today such that its endless stream is presented to us, its consumers, not for our benefit but for someone else's. This is something that everyone knows, however dimly.

Selling, now called "marketing," is one of the great concerns of contemporary social life at all levels, and accordingly so is *seeming*. Among other things this has given rise to industries focusing on packaging, branding, and reputation management, of both people and products. This marketing activity, as Frankfort says, may employ "exquisitely sophisticated craftsmen who—with the help of advanced and demanding techniques of market research, of public opinion polling, of psychological testing, and so forth—dedicate themselves tirelessly to getting every word and image they produce exactly right."[30] But the artistry is only a means to an end. Like their entire enterprise, they are "trying to get away with something" by pretending "to communicate the truth." Thus, to the extent that public relations, marketing, and advertising have become essential features of our culture, it is a culture of bullshit. In such a culture, even *sincerity* becomes a marketable political value, as was demonstrated by Barack Obama in 2008 and Bernie Sanders in 2016.

The brilliance of the marketers of the right—a Frank Luntz, say—must be countered by those on the left—a George Lakoff. But it is all bullshit. Bullshitting has become one of the essential cynical practices, reaching from simply advertising any new product[31] (as well as its design and development stages) to out-and-out political lies, as with Secretary of State Condoleezza Rice's threatened "mushroom cloud" selling the impending invasion of Iraq and being repeated endlessly as a "talking point."[32]

But perhaps it has always been true—emperors, priests, kings, the church, the aristocracy, the nation-state, the bourgeoisie have always commissioned the masters of communication to celebrate their rule and create appropriate propaganda, even spectacles. And hasn't the population always been manipulated in the interest of master cynics? There is a difference today. We are not subjects, but autonomous——indeed, educated and critically minded—citizens, no longer dominated by crude dogma and otherworldly beliefs under priestly oversight.

The leaders of government and industry are chosen to serve us, the citizens, and the economy is supposed to meet our needs. This is a democratic world, based on the free market and the consent of the governed, rather than on force or fear. This helps to explain the pervasiveness of cynicism: because we are free, and because our approval and our purchasing power rather than our submission or self-sacrifice are essential, we become the recipients of constant and pervasive appeals.[33]

Cynicism against Hope

Like hope, cynicism is frequently seen, incorrectly, as being an individual attitude. Like hope, it needs to be de-psychologized and stood on its legs in order to be properly understood both as a collective phenomenon and as a *practice*. More than that, today cynicism has a specific political coloration, as does hope. Although there are exceptions to this rule, "Nothing can be done about that" is a right-wing stance today, just as acting collectively is a left-wing stance.

Although "hopeful" right-wing activism has certainly mobilized around attacking and dismantling the fruits of past "progressive" collective activism—from welfare to banking regulation, from environmental protection to the union shop—the right/left divide generally fits when dealing with the environment, poverty, inequality, and public education. The right promotes cynicism about effecting improvement in these areas in which leftist hopes germinate.

Rephrasing Chaloupka, then, cynicism is both a way of life after the exhaustion of hope and, more to the point, a practice against hope. Anti-hope, cynicism is a determined passivity in the face of hopeful action. Today's cynicism creates and prizes isolated individuals who by definition cannot act together to solve problems. Of course cynics are correct to insist on facing the facts, but they do not see that the facts are created, not simply given, by human beings according to their own particular interests and against other interests. Thus there are always alternatives, and choices can always be made. Cynics also blind themselves to the history of unceasing collective efforts to create a better world, and the fact that those efforts have sometimes been successful and their results are sometimes cumulative. For all their pride in being enlightened, cynics demonstrate the appropriateness of Sloterdijk's original formulation, dooming them to wallow in false consciousness.

Whatever else it is, then, cynicism is a stance of denial. It assertively rejects hope, yes, and that broad stance entails the other meanings of *denying*, including refusing the facts, being unwilling to admit the reality of alternative possibilities, and depriving oneself. These are entailed by the experience of aloneness, which casts its shadows on everything within sight. Yet the cynical self of Cohen's song "Everybody Knows" is a socially produced self. The singer is quite eager to share his depressive sense that there is no alternative, but remains haunted by the deep knowledge that his lament is part of the problem and that the problem is a collective one.

Chapter 5

The Privatization of Hope

The recent rise of cynicism has been happening in connection with a wider process. We are living in the time of the privatization of hope. Throughout the world, but especially in the United States and the United Kingdom, a seismic shifting of aspirations and responsibilities is taking place, from the larger society to our own individual universes. The detaching of personal expectations from the wider world is transforming both beyond recognition. But why not simply use a term like "individualization" to characterize these processes, rather than the awkward-sounding "privatization of hope"? After all, individualization has already been the focus of considerable discussion among social theorists, starting with Anthony Giddens, Zigmunt Bauman, and Ulrich Beck, and making its way into the *New York Times*.[1] These and other writers have illuminated a dramatic historical shift toward the "risk society" or the "individualized society," or even a "second modernity."

My purpose in speaking of the "privatization of hope" is to claim both less and more for the process: to see it less as a matter of broad trends of social evolution while linking it explicitly to political, economic, and ideological projects of the past two generations, including the very deliberate construction of the consumer economy and then the turn toward neoliberalism. My formulation stresses a paradox: for most people in advanced societies today, especially in the United States and United Kingdom, hope—the realm of desires, expectations, and action—is already almost exclusively private. The term "the privatization of hope" is intended to call attention to itself, to challenge us to think about once social hopes that have been made private. It also calls attention to the fact that the processes I am describing may displace hope but do not kill it completely. We have not lost all hope over the past generation—indeed, we live amidst a maddening profusion of individual hopes. Under attack is the kind of hope that is social, the kind of collective coming together of movements that have struggled to make the world freer, more equal, more democratic, more livable. In their place something strange and remarkable has been happening as energies that once belonged to the social sphere have been transferred from there to one's personal life. Not only does this weaken collective capacities to solve collective problems, but the very sense of collectivity and the commons dissolves as the social sources of problems become hidden.

Even the relatively thin American notion of the common good is becoming replaced by a new individualism: sometimes assigning personal responsibility for the most obviously social functions; sometimes lost in a passive sense of fragmentation and isolation; sometimes crude, aggressive, even solipsistic. In a society that has always stressed individual self-reliance and responsibility, Americans seem less and less aware of how their paramount concern for their personal selves is intertwined with their social selves. Indeed, they are often unaware even of having a social self.

The Tea Party

The most stunning instance of this shift has been the eruption of the Tea Party in early 2009. By what political alchemy did the only movement generated during the first three years of the Great Recession demand more of the same policies that caused the crisis? The financial collapse of September 2008 refuted thirty years of deregulation and dismantling of the welfare state, but provoked few eruptions at the other end of the political spectrum, which was busy electing the new president and celebrating his victory but not pushing him on policy or giving him needed support. Still, wouldn't the next activist wave—after thirty-five years of top-down class struggle and increasing inequality—be a movement of the unemployed and foreclosed demanding collective action for jobs, relief, and punishment of the businessmen and speculators behind the financial collapse?

How bizarre then was the new wave of activists calling for even less government, even less regulation, even lower taxes, and an even flimsier safety net. Were these self-styled patriots in three-cornered hats simply out of touch with reality? Not with their reality: the Tea Party is a sour, middle- and upper-middle-class wave of resentment, comprising mostly college-educated white males over the age of forty-five, one-fifth of whom earn more than one hundred thousand dollars per year.[2] By what strange and twisted irony did the first mass mobilization with teeth since the New Left turn out to be the "libertarian mob" furious about the bailouts, rejecting any thought of helping the foreclosed?[3]

Indeed, the famous rant by a television announcer on February 19, 2009, angrily denounced those "losers" crying for federal aid as their mortgages went into default, and ridiculed subsidizing their "bad behavior."[4] In response to an urgent need for further government action to meet the crisis, and to the bank and auto bailouts and the Stimulus, Tea Party protests were organized to demand—no action at all. In the face of continuing massive unemployment, Tea Party supporters—clearly suffering far less than those from whom they would "take our country back"—demanded the right-wing media's talking points of lower taxes, less government, and reducing the Federal deficit.

The Tea Party's astonishing rise came in a matter of days and weeks after President Obama signed the Stimulus Act. A coalition of conservative activists launched demonstrations in eighty-one cities, claiming tens of thousands of participants, and the Tea Party riveted the attention of the mainstream media. After raising hell at the town meetings on health care reform and a massive national demonstration, Tea Partiers created a national electoral presence, winning primaries and then seats in Congress in the 2010 elections. A few years on, it has long since been thoroughly institutionalized as the activist core of the Republican Party, and the Tea Party exerts enormous pressure on political campaigns and public policy debates.

Yet this was a movement characterized from the start by wackiness, a distorted sense of history (and the Constitution), strangely misplaced anger, extreme rhetoric, and implicit racism. Think of the wild accusations about Obama's "socialism," the presence of guns and calls for revolution at Tea Party rallies, supporters' sympathy for weird claims by "birthers" that Obama was not born in the United States, and by others claiming that he was secretly a Muslim. Think of the "death panel" cries disrupting the town halls discussing the Democrats' health care proposals in 2009. And the rallying cry of taking "our" country back—Ours? From whom?—as well as their proud rejection of "elite" experts in their dismissal of climate change.

But was this phenomenon really a movement? Wasn't it rather a Potemkin village, or in more contemporary language an "Astroturf movement"—a "fake grassroots movement"?[5] After all, its spread would have been impossible without the instantly available deep pockets of funders such as the Koch brothers or Dick Armey's Freedomworks Foundation, or the years of inspiration, agitation, and now organization provided by right-wing media, especially Fox News.[6] From the beginning, the Tea Party was seized on both by the establishment media and by the various institutional forces on the right: colonized, organized, professionalized, manipulated, inflated, and thoroughly taken over by leading Republicans.[7] Still, it kept bubbling up from below.

The story of this furious outburst against social solidarity contains a remarkable irony. This movement of the right was in important ways fueled by the successes of the left during and since the 1960s, especially by the spread of freedom and equality. Since the social transformation of that era, the individual and his or her rights and responsibilities have come to count for far more than collective tasks such as combating global warming and eliminating poverty. With social transformation has come economic transformation: the expansion of consumer society, the proliferation of personal electronic devices, the growth of free market ideology, the defeat of alternatives to unregulated capitalism. All foster a scenario of detachment, in which each of us is free to ignore our sense of belonging to a larger society. Citizenship is being reduced to participation in regular elections that rarely offer genuine alternatives to the prevailing system, to moments of cheering for our side and honoring "our heroes." Even the collective action that remains is increasingly pitched in terms of the self-interest of millions of *me*'s.

The privatization of hope, then, is not simply a matter of turning inward to self and family. Giving up on a full sense of citizenship is also giving up on the greatest social hope of modernity—of democratically participating in shaping our world into a fit place in which to live.

The Privatization Movement

The Tea Party may have been instigated by the crisis of 2008–9, but many of its attitudes were generated during a generation-long attack on the welfare state and effort to reduce the size of government, as well as the undermining of public education. And gathering steam in every direction has been the privatization movement, the process in which socially owned and operated services and facilities have been turned over to private individuals and corporations, usually to be operated at a profit. The reasons given for this are usually the superior efficiency of private enterprise, the inefficiency of government, and the need to reduce costs; and behind these canards are economic interests expecting to benefit significantly from the ownership or operation of risk-free public services. But flowing from these, everywhere in the world, are militant ideological campaigns to dry up the public sphere and its sources of support, as well as a public mood of austerity expanded and deepened by fiscal crises. This wave has spread to mail services, water, prisons, wars, the military, police, schools, space exploration, transport, social security, public health services, and highways. During the Obama presidency, the mood of privatization and its projects only deepened. Think of Obama's "signature accomplishment": the only way a majority could be assembled to pass the social provision of health care was by basing the Affordable Care Act on the Republican idea of an individual mandate requiring citizens to purchase corporate insurance plans or pay a fine. In other words, Americans could begin to implement what they regarded as a fundamental right only insofar as it was already privatized.

A spiral of effects is set in motion by taking functions that belong properly to the community or the society, such as our schools, and turning them over to private agencies, businesses, or corporations. The common good that these functions embody is no longer experienced in common, and the individuals who receive the benefit of the privatized function do so no longer as citizens, but as consumers looking to get the best deal. The community still exists somewhere—indeed, it may still be providing in the abstract—but the concrete interaction goes on between private individuals as private individuals. Awareness that the community stands behind this becomes either minimized or ignored.

As we saw in the film *Waiting for Superman*, this project begins with animus against the public sphere and generates further animus. In a situation in which there is no longer any meaningful collective good, we witness the displacement from a shared condition to individual solutions. We experience the plight and hopes of those caring parents, and no other logic makes sense. The attack on public education diminishes everyone's sense of membership in the community, and strengthens their growing sense of being private individuals on the lookout only for themselves and their children. In fact, those who succeed in the political struggle to expand privatization are often allied with those who will provide the private service, and they do so by spreading hostility toward democratically decided public goods. In places such as Detroit, half of students attend charter schools created as privatized alternatives to the public system, which is fatally weakened by the loss of students and funding. And even this is not the last straw. That has come about in adjacent Highland Park, which closed its once outstanding high school and is down to a single public elementary school.

On One's Own

The privatization of hope is rooted in deep and wide processes of change since World War II. These changes are visible in landscapes and technologies, in work and leisure, and in people themselves. There has been a transformation of how and what people think, do, and feel.

One might object that in fact the changes I ascribe to the postwar era just continue an age-old trend. Indeed, as much of the history of Christianity demonstrates, rulers and their functionaries seek to divert people from the political and social conditions of their daily lives by encouraging them to assume personal responsibility for them. As I said in the previous chapter, a focus on personal responsibility, as Adam Smith and Karl Marx both knew, has been built into capitalism since its earliest moments.

But in the last generation this focus has developed in a way that can best be described by a term that is usually used medically: hypertrophy. Personal responsibility, and individualism more generally, have grown disproportionately, resembling an organ or body part that is excessively enlarged. As our culture grows more heavily influenced by psychology and therapy, as personal demands and technologies explode, and as individuals are increasingly fated to take control of their lives bounded by few traditional roles and customs, one is required to make endless decisions about one's education, job, place of residence, lifestyle, and family. "In the individualized society," Ulrich Beck writes, "the individual must therefore learn, on pain of permanent disadvantage, to conceive of himself or herself as the center of action, as the planning office with respect to his/ her own biography, abilities, orientations, relationships and so on."[8]

Of course the theme of being on one's own is deeply rooted in the history of a nation of immigrants. The uprooting processes that led to creating Americans, and the fact that the United States was the first entirely modern society, have always fostered a stronger sense of self-reliance here than in the old worlds most Americans emigrated from. This has entailed a fierce American commitment to individual freedom, including freedom from government interference (but not necessarily from government support and protection).

Yet American individualism did not rule out the brief flourishing of a mass socialist party nor, during the 1930s and after, major steps toward the creation of a social democratic welfare state. Both the socialist and social democratic movements were weaker in the United States than in other advanced societies, but during the civil rights years, President Lyndon Johnson declared a War on Poverty, Martin Luther King evolved toward embracing socialist ideas, and the Republican presidents Dwight Eisenhower and Richard Nixon fully endorsed the welfare state—strong signs that, as late as the 1970s, there was bipartisan room for collective solutions to collective problems.

In spite of Alexis de Tocqueville's concern that "individualism . . . disposes each member of the community to sever himself from the mass of his fellow creatures; and to draw apart with his family and friends"—that the individualist "willingly leaves society at large to itself"⁹—during the century and a half after his visit in the early 1830s, American citizenship flourished and expanded. A public-spirited citizenry pushed for emancipation, a massive trade union movement, civil rights for African Americans, expanded civil liberties, the separation of church and state, and two waves of a feminist revolution. In chapter 1, I mentioned the enormous range of public projects taking shape under the aegis of federal, state, and local governments. However individualist the society was, the production, preservation, and expansion of these public goods came to be seen as collective goals—sources of pride that expressed shared social values.

Granted, the collective was dominated by its wealthiest and most powerful members, corporate interests came to be more or less sacrosanct within it, and the "common good" has been marked by inequality and class, race, and gender domination, often bitterly contested. Even as these projects were underway, a strong streak of American mythology was celebrating the lone individual taking a dramatic stand against conformity, compromise, and corruption and often setting off westward, alone. But, Hollywood films and their escapist temptations aside, it was generally understood that the society's limitations would be corrected not by withdrawal but by deeper involvement: what was needed was a fairer and more just community, a New Deal, a Great Society, or even, as King suggested, a "better distribution of wealth," which in his view meant moving "toward a Democratic Socialism."

King's words remind us of the remarkable shift in the opposite direction that the last generation has been living through. Despite the individualism that only seemed to be intensified in the 1960s by the spread of automobiles, television, and the suburbs, under Lyndon Johnson not only were the civil rights laws passed, but Medicare and Medicaid came into existence and the nation launched its "War on Poverty." In individualist America, the sense of interconnectedness and social hope was strong enough in 1965 that almost half of Americans believed that government action would actually eliminate poverty!

It shows how far we have come, not only in the United States but also in other advanced societies, that such confidence appears unthinkable today, a naive relic of a bygone era. As David Whitman reported in *The Optimism Gap* (1998),[10] between 1959 and 1997, Americans' positive evaluation of their own present and future remained virtually unchanged, while their assessment of their society and its future, initially almost equal to the self-assessment, dropped by approximately twenty percentage points.[11]

This mood shift goes hand in hand with massive cultural changes. Detailed descriptions of the changes often include Europe as well as North America, and stretch from the latest pop-culture portrayals of new sensibilities to academic studies of evolving attitudes toward self and society, taking in the atomizing effects of the new "flexible capitalism" and its increasing inequality, as well as the effects of consumerism in intensifying of one's personal needs.[12] Of course it is tempting to exaggerate the changes and to trumpet each of them as announcing a new society or a new individual. Various efforts to describe this stress the different aspects of a generational shift: the hundred-year transformation of life in North America by the automobile, which did not merely privatize most daily transport but reshaped virtually everything in the land in its own image; the postwar decline of community and civic involvement, leading to people "bowling alone"; the more recent enlargement of the self, leading to an "epidemic of narcissism" and "generation me"; membership in the "individualized society" or the "risk society," where one is given full responsibility for one's life itinerary; the spread of neoliberal rationality and its "model of the market" to every area of life. And then there are the declarations that we have entered a new stage in the history of humanity in which our era of globalization and individualization, the one usually described as connected to the other, is proclaimed as being so far-reaching that it has initiated a "second modernity" or, less positively, a new era of "idiotism."

In their full-throated version each of these descriptions needs to be contested and corrected, but if we take them as alerting us to trends or tendencies, they point to an unmistakable cultural shift over the past fifty years. Individuals are freer than ever to live as they wish, to adopt or design precisely the religions, modes of behavior, and customs they wish. This is a world in which social energy in the advanced societies, especially in the United States and the United Kingdom, has been flowing less and less into collective social identities, projects, and satisfactions, and more and more into hundreds, thousands, millions of individual personal directions.

The question is: What changed? What caused the depletion not only of social goods but of social energy? Of not only the will to work together, but even the sense that togetherness could be politically, economically, and socially useful? Obviously there is no simple single answer, and searching for its causes must take us in a number of directions, beginning with the upheaval of the 1960s and the redefinition of roles and identities generated by the women's movement. Changes in the economy—including offshoring, deindustrialization, globalization, deregulation, and financialization—have impacted workers and owners, shrinking traditional ways of making a living and creating new ways of getting rich. Consumerism and the pursuit of profit have burrowed ever more deeply into the society, indeed the world, and a culture has been created that places the "bottom line" at its center. These trends find their way into individuals, entailing an expansion and distortion of personal responsibility, including one for social processes not under individual control. The more responsible individuals become for their fate, including their life choices and identities, the fewer ties they have to their place, their society, and their world. Capping all these changes, and helping to drive them, has been a relentless ideological campaign for individual responsibility and against collective action.

Just to mention these forces is to bow toward the many studies being done on these themes. Drawing on some of this work, in the remainder of this chapter I will sketch in greater detail some of the main causes of the privatization of hope: the 1960s attack on traditional social roles and stress on personal liberation, "flexible capitalism," consumerism, "inventing oneself," constant migration, the neoliberal project of "changing the soul."

The 1960s Origins of Privatized Hope

Whereas today society is besieged by individuals, in the 1950s and early '60s individuals felt besieged by the society. For the generation coming to consciousness in the '60s, Allen Ginsberg's *Howl* (1955) reflected the oppressed individual, as did Herbert Marcuse's *One-Dimensional Man* (1964). Each author described a social system that stifled any alternatives to its values and dominant practices, and each gave ammunition to those seeking ways out.

The early New Left—as exemplified by the Student Nonviolent Coordinating Committee, the Free Speech Movement, Students for a Democratic Society, and the women's movement—was in many ways a response to the situation Ginsberg and Marcuse described. Convinced that the personal was political, many in the New Left placed individual needs and experience at the center of their rebellion and emphasized participatory democracy. Both projects militated against the dominant culture and became components of a counterculture expressed in long hair, casual dress, drug experimentation, sexual freedom, and an explosion of new music. Even as it separated into two currents—one more political and the other more countercultural—the wave of the '60s never stopped pushing individual liberation. This feature of the New Left and its centrality in the much wider counterculture has led otherwise astute observers such as Mark Lilla and Tony Judt to ignore the movement's organized and disciplined commitment to social justice, and to reduce the '60s to an era of do-your-own-thing individualism.[13]

The political activism of the New Left accelerated revolutionary, if unfinished, change: women's liberation, gay liberation, the overthrow of segregation in the American South, and the broader attack on racism in the advanced world. But there is another side to these changes, which points to the paradox of the New Left. As I suggested above, these movements of emancipation have had an individualizing and privatizing effect.[14] In making the personal political, and pushing self-esteem—e.g., "black is beautiful"—they have heightened the personal while distancing people from the political.

For example, the women's movement has achieved greater freedom and equality than ever before, and this has generated an ongoing transformation of the institution of marriage, of male-female relations, and, in tandem with the liberation of gays and lesbians, of the whole realm of family relations and how society governs them. Traditional roles and norms have been upended, individuals are inventing their own models, and no one quite knows what to do or how to think.

Fortunately, help is not far away. On any life issue, an array of experts stands ready to offer advice, helping us to work our way through confusing terrain. Take for example, "How to Recognize Dating Deal Breakers." This article in the *Chicago Tribune* interviews four experts. One of these is the proprietor of the "#1 free Q & A advice forum where over 20,000 questions have been asked and answered by nearly 200,000 members; she has more than 620,000 Facebook fans and over 1.4 million Twitter followers." Another expert is the founder of a dating website who asks new clients to "list their top five must-haves, nice-to-haves and cannot haves" when they sign up. A third, a psychologist, asks people to focus on three or four significant personal differences with one's romantic attachment, and advises couples to discuss whether or how they might be negotiated. And the fourth, a clinical hypnotherapist, similarly asks people to focus on "what matters most to you in love and life." What emerges in this article are "relationship tips: when to compromise and end it," based on an in-depth personal exploration of "what you can or can't accept for a relationship to continue."[15] This entails the process of "reflexivity" described by Giddens, the contemporary world's constant process of self-creation and self-monitoring, generating an ongoing sense of who you are and who the other person is.

A recent Google search under "relationship advice" turned up well over five million hits, many of them no doubt from similar would-be relationship counselors. Unlike the patriarchal ideologists described in Barbara Ehrenreich and Deirdre English's *For Her Own Good*, presumably few of these counselors offers wisdom with social authority, as an elder might have done in the past, but each expert presents him- or herself as a technician helping you to understand the practical consequences of ignoring your own personal limits or "must-haves," and passing no moral judgements on whatever those may be. Above all, it is important to be aware of deal breakers: "The most common deal breakers people cite include smoking, drug use, financial troubles, infidelity and not wanting children."

However, in addition to replacing the patriarchal advice-giving functions of the past with a freer, less repressive orientation based on the individual's own needs and feelings, as Ehrenreich and English point out, the relationship advice industry signals a no less significant shift. Feminism was once concerned with social change, demanding child care, parental leave, flexible work schedules, "and all the necessities of a life that would allow women and men to benefit equally from a balance between work and home." But these community-building energies have been diverted into searching for individualistic solutions. These ignore difficult realities women face concerning time, income, single-parenting, discrimination, and the absence of social support. "There is no justification for mutual help or social change in an ideology that assumes each person is wholly responsible for her own condition: every individual must break out alone."[16] Alone, women "wander the aisle of the same Great American Advice Mall without necessarily ever seeing one another."[17]

Privatized Hope in the World of Work

The theme of individual freedom has been central to the dramatic shift of political, economic, and cultural power known as neoliberalism. Since the '70s, advanced societies have promoted a globalized, information-driven capitalist offensive accompanied by a new social model based on what historian Steve Fraser describes as "the heroism of risk." The daring of entrepreneurs and Wall Street—the latter often false because it is underwritten by the government—gilds them with a special glow of boldness, such that these forces of the status quo become, ironically, models of rebellion: "Entrepreneurs are rule-breakers by nature," an editorial in a recent issue of *Entrepreneur* magazine declares. "They disrupt, innovate and feel damn good about it."[18] Never mind that the true revolution is in the lives of average workers who find they can no longer count on job stability. Hallmarks of the new capitalism, insecure working conditions place a premium on preparing oneself for the next move and the move after that, rather than allowing workers to settle into long-term relationships that might enable group protection against employers. In Fraser's words, the neoliberal economy allows corporations to "nourish a lively sense that work is undertaken at will by free agents,"[19] making it seem as if "the world as reconstituted by flexible capitalism has given birth to the free-floating individual: unmoored from all those ties of kin, home, locale, race, ethnicity, church, craft, and fixed moral order, her only home is the marketplace furnished in unforgiving arithmetic. Her selfhood is that of the abstract, depersonalized fungible commodity, a homunculus of rationalizing self-interest."[20]

Today, rather than work alongside others, a condition that once produced a sense of solidarity, labor is increasingly individualized, compensated for by the "freedom" to change jobs frequently, be responsible for oneself, and work at home. Flexible capitalism has created the temporary work world of the "precariat," whose freedom lacks what painfully and over time had become the customary working conditions: health care benefits, pensions, vacation and sick days, and "any possibility of effectively voicing [one's] displeasure in the workplace."[21]

Thrown on the market as isolated individuals without collective support from unions or government, fated to "move on" and "reinvent oneself" frequently during their lifetimes, workers face the constant need to market and package themselves by developing salable qualifications through training. At one time, workers understood that they could improve their conditions by collectively asserting themselves; now workers understand that their best option is to protect themselves *by themselves*. Among self-seekers, experiences of class and solidarity are impossible and irrelevant. As Fraser says, when the self is the only viable site of betterment, when there is no possible gain from collective action, collective consciousness seems "foolish, naive, woolly-headed or, on the contrary, sinful and seditious."

Consumerism

Alongside changing cultural politics and the erosion of work-place stability, consumerism has been a principal source of the postwar privatization of hope. Suburbanization and the boom in private automobile travel brought a new level of comfort to Americans' lives in the late 1940s and '50s. With these things came a strong orientation toward material possessions—purchased to fill those homes, easily shuttled from distant shops—fostered more successfully than ever by their manufacturers. In the previous chapter we saw Galbraith's 1958 claim that the producer has the "function both of making the goods and of making the desires for them." Desire is "synthesized by advertising, catalyzed by salesmanship, and shaped by the discreet manipulations of the persuaders."

The endless and intensive stimulation of individual "needs" cannot help but divert the individual's focus from collective needs and aspirations. And the increasing cultural priority given to the consumer role cannot help but turn one away from seeing and experiencing oneself collectively. The social role of the consumer does entail collective belonging and participation, but only insofar as one is exposed to advertising as the others are, one compares one's own acquisitions with others, and one joins others in purchasing new goods. This is why Galbraith insisted that "consumer sovereignty" is a myth; it hides the absence of control over the most basic conditions of one's life. Choosing consumer goods is structurally different from the role of union member or citizen in that the social energies of consumer society, and the wealth it produces and consumes, are destined for individuals *as* individuals, whose primary function is to shop for themselves.

One need only go to a baseball game to become part of the spectacle of consumer society. The role of the consumer *as a distinctive way of being* differs markedly from that of the baseball fan of fifty years ago. On the field, the sport appears roughly the same as ever, which is part of its charm. Yet to participate as a fan today means entering a paradise of consumerism. The audience comes into the stadium mostly wearing the specially purchased clothes of the home team. They have been prepared for the game by endless newspaper, Internet, radio, and television coverage of every aspect of the team's ups and downs. These include unenlightening interviews with the players, manager, and coaches, and vigorous fan participation and commentary online and via talk shows. Nearly all of the players, especially the "free agents," make obscene salaries; many sign lucrative endorsement contracts; and almost none have local roots. Nevertheless, from the fans' standpoint, they are "our" team. During the game itself, the fans are subjected to hundreds of advertisements, both fixed and changing, mounted everywhere one turns; videos and live promotions flashing on the scoreboard; and inane sponsored contests between innings. The walk to the concessions and toilets is a tour through an immense shopping mall. All of this commercialism aside, the active, collective aspect of watching a ball game—spontaneously mounting group cheers and chants for one's team during exciting moments—has been virtually eliminated by programmed cheers emanating from the scoreboard and speaker system.

Attending a baseball game reveals that consumer society has not developed new social and political forms, and that many of its activities remain continuous with what came before. The game, after all, is the reason why people go to the ballpark. But in key respects its content is strikingly different: the consumer-oriented media spectacle influences the fans' priorities, activities, values and attitudes. Whatever the game's earlier and even continuing functions, it more and more takes place within the mass society of nonstop marketing and shopping.

Galbraith suggested that the main force behind this transformation is the need of corporations to stimulate demand. How did this come about historically? In one step after another, consumers were asked to choose, by the tens and eventually hundreds of millions, to purchase the expanding range of available goods. But they had to become disposed to do so. Creating this disposition meant, first of all, overcoming the traditional desire among workers to work less rather than consume more. In ostensibly democratic societies, this decision in favor of more consumption rather than less work was never made democratically. Certainly from the '50s on, there was much discussion of automation, including its promise of a shorter workweek. But such proposals received little support in Congress and never became part of a broad public discussion about alternatives. Instead, the logic of consumer society prevailed: greater productivity meant expanding consumer goods and no decrease in working hours. Today even that promise seems all but gone, as increasing workers' productivity without sharing the increasing profit has become one of management's goals. The dominant social reality of our time, the consumer society, was not so much chosen as imposed by the logic of the capitalist economy.

It is understandable that masses of people who had endured grating poverty since time immemorial would want to enjoy the available plenty and its convenience, comfort, and luxury. But, in the long run, consumerism could never have developed to its essential place in advanced societies without negotiating two other zones of resistance. In the first were the traditional values of moderation and postponement of gratification, hallmarks of scarcity supported throughout history by religious and cultural values. The consumer society has generated a sea change in the culture by reversing all such injunctions and instead promoting hedonism and instant gratification.

The other barrier to expanding consumerism was consumers' limited income, to which the unrestrained expansion of credit, especially in North America, became the answer. Credit cards in the purse or wallet freed consumers from old-fashioned inhibitions: living in a brilliant world of media brought to us by corporate sponsors, why not indulge desires, which in this environment have become needs?

Inventing Oneself

A result and further cause of the privatization of hope is the growing tendency for individuals to see themselves entrepreneurially, as agglomerations of social capital. Wendy Brown describes this as an aspect of the wholesale reshaping of social life in economic terms in the neoliberal universe. Related to this is the encouragement and pressure for individuals to construct their lives consciously and deliberately in the form of a biography. I have suggested that the process of self-invention and reinvention is drawn in the first place from conditions prevailing in the workplace and its demand for constant self-marketing. Beyond this, however, some of its sharpest formulations come from psychotherapy and its injunction to take command of our lives and become the active subjects of our own stories.

Privatization of the social is an essential part of this process. It would be hard to disagree with Marx that one's story is never wholly one's own, that lives are not made "under self-selected circumstances, but under circumstances existing already, given and transmitted from the past."[22] But we can, and do, ardently pretend. As Zygmunt Bauman describes:

> The distinctive feature of the stories told in our times is that they articulate individual lives in a way that excludes or suppresses (prevents from articulation) the possibility of tracking down the links connecting individual fate to the ways and means by which society as a whole operates; more to the point, it precludes the questioning of such ways and means by relegating them to the unexamined background of individual life pursuits and casting them as "brute facts" which the story-tellers can neither challenge nor negotiate, whether singly, severally or collectively.[23]

Bauman continues:

> With the supra-individual factors shaping the course of an individual life out of sight and out of thought, the added value of "joining forces" and "standing arm in arm" is difficult to spot, and the impulse to engage (let alone engage critically) with the way the human condition, or the shared human predicament, is shaped is weak or non-existent.[24]

The author of a book entitled *Codependent No More* advises her readers: "The surest way to make ourselves crazy is to get involved with other people's businesses, and the quickest way to become sane and happy is to tend to our own affairs."[25] The message of the "therapeutic gospel" is to focus on one's own pleasure and happiness with a clear conscience. The emphasis on "taking control of one's life" contributes to the process of desocialization and desolidarization. It also points toward the displacement of hope. When individuals become personally responsible for these problems, social pain and its causes are conjured away. The energy to resolve them remains, though, and a manic sense of empowerment results—one that is bound to be frustrated without our understanding why. Displaced onto individuals, hope takes on the aspect of an addiction that can never be satisfied.

In becoming fated to seek, in Beck's words, "biographic solutions for systemic contradictions,"[26] people lose track of their social being. "As a result," Beck says, "the floodgates are opened wide for the subjectivization and individualization of risks and contradictions produced by institutions and society."[27] To be sure, one does become increasingly aware of living one's biography in world society, and active "thinking individuals" who have "to take a continual stand" are increasingly in demand. Ironically, as the individual becomes more and more insignificant, his or her sense of self expands, and, from the biographical point of view, "he or she is elevated to the apparent throne of a world-shaper."[28] World society enters biography, but "this continual excessive demand can only be tolerated through the opposite reaction of not listening, simplifying, and apathy." And so the focus on oneself deepens further.

Paradoxically, this expanded self-as-entrepreneur is an impoverished self, less and less concerned with the development of knowledge, interests, and capacities, and more and more obsessed, as Brown describes it, with "maximizing competitiveness." For example, the modern world once promised education as including the development of the intellect and the capacity for citizenship, but this has given way almost completely to education in terms of "capital appreciation and investment."[29] If neoliberalism encourages the privatization of hope, the individual thereby produced is in fact a narrow one. The goal is no longer a full, many-sided individual, nor is education "sought for developing the capacities of citizens, sustaining culture, knowing the world, or envisioning and crafting different ways of life in common."

Leaving Detroit

Another effect and further cause of such narrowing of one's horizons is the massive migration that, in the past fifty years, has depopulated some American cities while creating others. Of course, migration is one of the major themes of history—of groups large and small, of families and individuals, seeking food and land, fleeing from war, escaping oppression, running from threatening people, hoping to overcome deprivation, seeking opportunity. And the motivations for leaving Detroit have been very much the same: insecurity, discomfort at being in the minority, dwindling property values, deteriorating neighborhoods and schools, high levels of crime, lack of economic opportunity following the flight or collapse of industry. This migration was also underpinned by Americans' nomadic disposition, which, from the beginning, has led to their formulating their hopes in individual terms and then moving on as a location became played out.

Still, it is hard to avoid the sense that something novel is happening when one drives past mile after ghastly mile of empty storefronts and vacant lots, block after block each with one or two occupied houses separated by wild grass and weeds and an occasional garden; when stable neighborhoods celebrate their "stayers"; and when one contemplates the staggering reality that more than a million people have left Detroit for the suburbs, and that at least that many have left the metropolitan area and Michigan for newer cities and sunnier places. True, they have been pursuing their personal hopes, but their hundreds of thousands of individual decisions to give up on Detroit have added up to a collective abandonment, worsening the city's problems and driving it into bankruptcy. This is not to mention the concerted social policy to create charter schools. Aren't the desultory public efforts at renewal, rebuilding, and revitalization in the face of this hemorrhaging testimony that in twenty-first century America only the private matters?

Privatization and Power

At a very deep level, the displacement from the social to the individual, the growth of the personal at the expense of the social, and the remaking of the social into the biographical are all shaped by relations of power and domination, and these are tied to the overwhelming force exerted on every aspect of our being by the economy and its priorities. Under these conditions, basic social impulses such as the need to contribute to a wider community become other than themselves without completely losing their original character, which abides in a repressed form. We can imagine a rebalancing of the social and the personal as a kind of "return of the repressed," but only in response to a transformation of the economic order that has been driving it.

In the past generation that order has imposed a deliberate ideological and political project aiming to erode social connectedness and conviction. The first politician seeking to implement the renewed Hobbesianism was British Prime Minister Margaret Thatcher. "There is no such thing as society, only individuals and families," she famously declared, in what turned out to be a prophecy of this transformation. Thatcher stressed that economics was only a method, but that "the object is to change the soul." A generation later in the United Kingdom, the United States, and elsewhere, dramatic historical changes have been doing just that: redefining the self, who learns to treat the world beyond his or her own skin in new ways.

In part this has resulted from an immensely effective, well organized, and lavishly funded effort to reshape values, ideas, and attitudes. Writers working for right-wing think tanks such as the Cato Institute and the Heritage Foundation have implored us to turn away from treating the public realm as a terrain for improvement and change. They have been preaching cynicism about collective action and instead encouraging individual responsibility, personal initiative, and the centrality of private activities. The influence that these cynical messages enjoy may, perversely, be a product of the well-being supported by the Western welfare states. In *Ill Fares the Land*, Judt writes:

> The success of the mixed economies of the past half century has led a younger generation to take stability for granted and to demand the elimination of the "impediment" of the taxing, regulating, and generally interfering state. This discounting of the public sector has become the default political language in much of the developed world.[30]

The comfortable citizens of these welfare states, David Harvey writes, have proved easy prey to "rhetoric about individual freedom, liberty, personal responsibility and the virtues of privatization, the free market and free trade,"—rhetoric that legitimizes the "draconian policies designed to restore and consolidate capitalist class power" that waned during the three and half decades of social democracy.

Following Michel Foucault rather than Harvey, Brown depicts these shifts in terms that are wider and deeper, although still inseparable from the evolution of capitalism. We have already seen her say that individual and collective control of the conditions under which we live is being renounced.

> The neoliberal solution to problems is always more markets, more complete markets, more perfect markets, more financialization, new technologies, new ways to monetize. Anything but collaborative and contestatory human decision making, control over the conditions of existence, planning for the future; anything but deliberate constructions of existence through democratic discussion, law, policy. Anything but the human knowledge, deliberation, judgment, and action classically associated with *Homo politicus*.[31]

As economic logic becomes the dominant, indeed the only social logic, collective power, collective decision making, the public, the community—all become further privatized. In the world of privatized hope, "the individual," "choice," "economic freedom," and "individual liberty" are proclaimed as clear and self-evident truths. The fetish for market solutions to all social problems is based on the fantasy, outlined by the Cato Institute's David Boaz, that "order in society arises spontaneously, out of the actions of thousands or millions of individuals who coordinate their actions with those of others in order to achieve their purposes."[32] Is this an unconscious appeal to a higher power? In any case, in ignoring the inequalities within this free play of individual actions, or those that governments do indeed coordinate, or the crying need for greater collective action on behalf of the common good, it is a posture of denial.

After all, what must command our attention is not the radical falsity of the privatization of hope, but its debilitating consequences. We are losing the collective ability to cope with the most urgent problems. People who see themselves as random, isolated individuals will never find the wherewithal to understand or agree upon, let alone master, the reality of climate change. The increasingly dangerous effect of two centuries of uncoordinated actions can be brought under control only if we accept that there is an *us* that has transformed nature and our relationship to it.[33] To protect our common home from disaster, humans must form a responsive global collective. We must recover and enlarge social hope in the name of survival. But how to do this if a critical mass lacks the capacity to see itself socially?

Our need, according to the French social theorist Francis Jeanson, is for "citoyennisation"—the transformation of isolated and impotent individuals into active, militant citizens who experience their fate collectively and are willing to act on it together.[34] Only if isolated individuals come to experience themselves and act as citizens is it possible to overcome the present fragmented, cynicism-driven determination to keep avoiding the issues convulsing the earth. This book's next question, then, is this: In a universe of shrinking social hope, what are our capacities for once again experiencing ourselves collectively?

Chapter 6

We

The contemporary afflictions we have explored—the maelstrom of economic progress, pervasive cynicism, and the privatization of hope—are so many reasons why people are less likely to mobilize themselves into movements. But can we take heart from any countertrends? What is the evidence for an alternative? Are there, in other words, reasons for social hope?

For one thing, we must not get carried away by today's lie, the lie of the *I*, and not give it too much credibility. We are besieged by a false individualism today, just as previous generations elsewhere were besieged by a false collectivism. Of course each of us is an *I*, and history has rightly discarded the lie of the *we* incarnated in the Soviet Union, which proclaimed the priority of a tyrannically imposed collectivity over its individuals. Nevertheless, despite the recent currents of privatization and individualization, one of the bases for social hope today remains what it always was: our fundamentally collective existence.

To experience this we must free ourselves from the effects of Margaret Thatcher's attack on social belonging, which proclaimed not merely a politician's slogan but a remarkably successful intellectual, economic, social, and political project to transform how people think and feel. Was she able to "change the soul"? The truth is that—despite the formidable social energy invested in it; despite its implementation in the remaking of economic, educational, cultural, and psychological realities; despite the rational choice philosophies that came to dominate academic disciplines such as economics and political science; despite even the physical realities of communities and consumer products that further separate people—the individualism they proclaim is fundamentally false. It distorts rather than explains economic reality and the nature of individuals themselves; it distorts morality, and is incoherent as a political and social goal.

But how can this be—especially when, as we've just seen, individualism is the order of the day, and privatization reflects one of the most powerful social trends? As I asked concerning progress, how can what is undeniably real be false?

Every generation and every individual is situated within human society and its vast network of historically created skills, structures, processes, institutions that constitute the nonbiological infrastructure of human life. Contrary to current ideology, we are raised within society, and through it we develop consciousness, language, fundamental skills, and access to its specific tools, built environment, and culture. Through it, we become individuals. Despite today's virtual prohibition against historical thinking, whoever and wherever we are, we start from where those who came before us left off, our lineage of development stretching back to early humans learning to use fire and migrating from Africa, and forward to particular peoples, nations, religious and ethnic groups, classes, and families in their collective and individual struggles to live and be treated more decently. It is no less profound for being a truism: All of this history is indeed our story. Our sociality is the very core of our identity as individuals.

Our social dependence not only reaches into the past, and to the most basic steps of humans creating themselves, but is alive at every moment in the present. Our daily survival and functioning depend on dozens, hundreds, thousands of links, assumed in our most personal decisions. We belong to families, and through them to obvious structures, networks, and processes of work, friends, neighborhood, city, and nation, as well as the natural environment—and to a social universe of which we usually remain unconscious. If we focus our awareness on how structures and networks and processes are actualized around the world, we may eventually notice those whose work daily makes us and our lives possible, just as our work in some small way contributes to making them and their lives possible. The being of any individual partakes of this vast human map, drawing its colors from infrastructures and technologies, economic and social structures. In our survival and in every activity we are utterly dependent on people, relationships, and structures everywhere in the world, and these too can be mapped.

Sartre denied that society was a "hyperorganism" operating with an independent force that could not be explained by the activity of the individuals comprising it. But he insisted that the active and deliberate social groupings that come into being stem not from some preexisting conscious, unified *we* that can be rendered in capital letters, but rather from the latent capacity of individual social beings to join together collectively. In this sense *we*, the group in fusion, is a project, not an entity.

When mobilized, as Sartre shows, *we* can act with enormous force, but *we* is also fragile and temporary. In time, as the history of the Paterson silk strike demonstrates, it may dissolve back into its separate individuals. Or, as Sartre described in *Critique of Dialectical Reason*, the mobilized individuals may seek to preserve the group by institutionalizing it. Even at its most thinglike and oppressive, however, the constituted institution can always be understood in terms of the original project and intentions that have brought it into being.[1]

The point is that even if it is only latent in our experience, in some sense slumbering, deemphasized and virtually ignored, our social being has the potential to be activated as a powerful force. The previous chapter in this book focused on some of the processes that cloud our awareness of this side of ourselves. They obscure it but cannot efface it: today more than ever it is our social belonging that connects us from the local to the global, that imposes individualization and privatization on us.[2] The great paradox of our social life is that we live the phenomena of globalization, noticing, for example, our food from Peru, Mexico, Australia and a dozen regions of the United States; our clothing from Albania, Macau, Mauritius, Honduras, Poland, and Sri Lanka; and our household objects from China, Vietnam, South Africa, and Kenya—but we do not usually see ourselves as fully social. As the world and our own selves are organized, our various kinds of social belonging are experienced passively, serially, since we live them as the result of large and uncontrollable forces rather than reciprocally and interactively. We experience our social being as consumers rather than subjects, as spectators rather than as agents, as products rather than producers, as isolated individuals rather than as groups.

In part this is because since the 1960s there has been a riotous proliferation of freedoms, amenities, and lifestyles: tattoos and pornography, the Internet and smart phones, psychotherapy for all, self-esteem and the constant need to hear and say "I love you," coffee houses and art fairs, T-shirts and jeans, oral sex and divorce, the niche economy and nonstop entertainment, a thousand kinds of music and dozens of ways of gaining access to it, huge interest in gourmet food and wines, cruises and travel everywhere, yoga and working out, eating out several times a week, fantasy sports, Twitter and Facebook, Whole Foods and Trader Joe's, "your comments" online about everything under the sun, reality TV and shows about cooking, real estate, and home remodeling. . . . The list reflects the kaleidoscopic and immensely profitable expansion of choice, consumer goods, entertainment, and individual expressiveness in our lifetimes. The space in which individuals move today in advanced societies and sectors everywhere is far more comfortable, freer, far more inclusive, far more interesting and diverse, more tolerant, and humanly and socially far richer than anyone would have imagined upon closing the pages of Herbert Marcuse's *One-Dimensional Man* or Allen Ginsberg's *Howl* fifty years ago.

Why would anyone want to rebel against this or shrink it in any way? These are important human acquisitions, due in part to the ways in which human actors, including some of us, have since the 1960s resisted repressions and responded to the possibilities within and around us. Yet what a paradox: we have significantly changed ourselves, others, and the world, fighting for and winning diversity, tolerance, and freedom, but we haven't challenged or changed the most important thing of all. Standing behind and overseeing, and thus decisively shaping, all of our newfound capacities and pleasures is the capitalist system itself. Revolutionary in many ways, the new energies released since the 1960s have become vital new sources of its expansion and profits. Indeed, capitalists have proven that they can be so hip and tolerant that, among young people today, we have seen that being an entrepreneur has some of the same cultural cachét as political activism had in an earlier time.

Countertrends

Accordingly, activating our deep social being from its latent state may depend on trends that run counter to the main directions of social life. And we can certainly see such trends, beginning at least with the alter-globalization movements and thinkers, including the various World Social Forums that have drawn together hundreds of thousands in search of solidarity and common strategies for responding to capitalist globalization under the slogan "Another world is possible." In the wake of the financial crisis of 2008 and the Great Recession that followed, the Occupy movements were conceived in a similar spirit and managed to create, while they lasted, functioning oppositional communities in full view and on public spaces. They rejected the importance of leadership and operated according to new forms of participatory democracy. And their spread dramatically showed a striking feature of the kinds of social hope described in chapter 2: how it can become contagious and mobilize millions around the world on behalf of similar goals.

In the aftermath of the Great Recession, we have also seen the development of political movements and parties that draw upon and activate our social being. These movements broke with the realism of all other established parties, as did the stunning growth of the Bernie Sanders presidential candidacy in the United States and Jeremy Corbyn's shocking victory as the leader of the Labour Party in the United Kingdom. For the first time in generations, a major American politician explicitly spoke about and to the working class, and referred to himself as a socialist. For the first time ever, a major American politician focused on inequality and concretely pitched his campaign to the concerns of young people. Sanders's relative silence about foreign policy issues indicates that he knew well that he was operating within strict limits, but nevertheless the rise of both Sanders and Corbyn speaks to a widespread rejection of cynicism about politics. As the political commentator D. D. Guttenplan wrote in *The Nation*, the two men shared "a reputation for putting principle ahead of popularity, a willingness to challenge their own party's conventional wisdom—especially on the economy—and an improbable status as icons of authenticity in an age of sound-bite politics."[3]

A related countertrend concerns the environmental movement. Despite the self-defeating compromises by "realistic" mainstream environmental groups duly noted by Naomi Klein, she also registers the growing radicalism of both individuals and groups, exemplified by the fact that her call for a transformation of capitalism and the end of economic growth as we know it, *This Changes Everything: Capitalism versus the Climate*, has been translated into over thirty languages and has more than a million copies in print. More dramatic yet is the appearance on the scene of Pope Francis, with his no less radical call for uniting liberation theology and environmentalism. Indeed, Francis goes so far as to call for an end to progress as we know it. His

"On Care for Our Common Home" is worth quoting at length because it shows how far he has stepped out of the mainstream commitment to progress, as well as the way in which ecopolitics speaks to the truth of social, not individual, being.

> For new models of progress to arise, there is a need to change "models of global development";[136] this will entail a responsible reflection on "the meaning of the economy and its goals with an eye to correcting its malfunctions and misapplications."[137] It is not enough to balance, in the medium term, the protection of nature with financial gain, or the preservation of the environment with progress. Halfway measures simply delay the inevitable disaster. Put simply, it is a matter of redefining our notion of progress. A technological and economic development which does not leave in its wake a better world and an integrally higher quality of life cannot be considered progress. Frequently, in fact, people's quality of life actually diminishes—by the deterioration of the environment, the low quality of food or the depletion of resources—in the midst of economic growth. In this context, talk of sustainable growth usually becomes a way of distracting attention and offering excuses. It absorbs the language and values of ecology into the categories of finance and technocracy, and the social and environmental responsibility of businesses often gets reduced to a series of marketing and image-enhancing measures.[4]

Like much environmentalism, these thoughts rest on a deep understanding of our social being as well as a rejection of acquisitive individualism. The earth and its climate are our *commons*, belonging to no one and everyone, to the future as well as the present.

Several other things about "On Care for Our Common Home" are important for us. Through it the pope is joining and enormously amplifying the forces of radical environmentalism. In so doing, he is bringing into the mainstream the call for an end to the civilizational commitment to progress that stems from profit-driven economic growth. And by speaking against increasing inequality, he is connecting the dots between the environment and the poor, who are made to bear the greatest burdens imposed by the current stage of civilization.

We do not know how these developments affect those who are more or less socially unaware and uninvolved. But when they are asked questions that require an answer from the social side of their being, massive numbers of ordinary people commonly say that something has gone wrong. There are obvious reasons anyone might call to mind: senseless consumerism, climate change, increasing inequality, increasing organization of childhood to prepare the young for a life of competition, undermining of democracy by the 1 percent. Little wonder that responses to the regular US polling question "Are you satisfied with the direction of our country?" have been negative for more than a generation, with the exception of a few brief moments.[5]

Taken together, these various countertrends indicate significant dissatisfaction with the status quo, and they suggest that transformative movements are possible. Of course such movements will have to contend with the new relations of power that have emerged over the past generation—which is why Sanders spoke of a "political revolution." Austerity, neoliberalism, the shrinking of welfare states, the growth of inequality, and deregulation have been possible only because of a changing balance of forces in which capitalism has expanded as a social, political, and cultural force. For all our many movements, in the United States there is not yet any large and coherent countervailing force—no longer can this be found in trade unions, churches, or in traditional habits or values. After the Great Recession, which was brought about by the uncontrolled financialization of the American and British economies, the same processes and institutions that caused the collapse have continued to rule with not even the briefest pause, and when Occupy finally emerged three years later it faded within a few months without even beginning to sketch a programmatic alternative or even a set of demands. The movement sparked by the Sanders candidacy for president began to do so, and its future is very much open. The most powerful countermovement anywhere, Syriza, rose to power in Greece but within months was crushed by the financial might of the European Union, the International Monetary Fund, and the European Central Bank.

Changing Our Point of View

Conventional wisdom on the left says that any hopeful conclusions to be drawn from the positive countertrends and history of successful organizing must be balanced with a realistic assessment of limits. Taken together, such analyses might give us an understanding of the possibilities for change. But necessary as it is, this kind of calculus can only take us so far. A leap is still needed, pivoting from studying our situation to acting on it. Only then do we alight on the terrain of hope.

Even if the analyses yield a thin margin of optimism, including genuine reasons for hope, they are not the stuff of hope itself. For a time it can seem the most urgent thing in the world to spell out reasons for hope, as I have just been doing, but after a while it seems utterly beside the point—hope takes shape, after all, when people act. To get the taste of hope today we must shift our point of view entirely. In chapter 2 I described the various ontological, psychological, and epistemological changes in perspective that accompany collective action. The act of creating change with others changes who we are, carrying us well beyond objectively analyzing possibilities.

This process carries a few theoretical considerations with it. In chapter 4 I mentioned that in Leonard Cohen's "Everybody Knows," the singer, the song, and the audience become part of the problem. There is a self-critical edge to the complicity offered by the song, and thus it necessarily undermines its own cynicism. I pointed out that specific forms of cynicism can be stages on the way to creating movements of change. Millions of individuals feel unable to do anything about the situation, which is presented as an unchangeable fact; but lamenting our collective impotence may reveal that impotence is an attitude as much as anything else, and owning it as *ours* can lead to the possibility of *we* coming together to act.

This is because hope, is not so much a philosophical concept or a feeling or even an attitude as it is a unique combination of the subjective and the objective. When the objective is overemphasized, the subjective must be brought back into the conversation, and vice versa. Throughout this book I've been stressing hope as the collective disposition to act politically, particularly on behalf of left-wing causes, and to do so under propitious conditions. We act on the possibility that history is smiling on us—that is, in circumstances in which our goals may actually be realized. This hope is neither a wholly subjective dimension of life nor a movement of events governed by iron laws. It is potency and possibility.

Marx, so keen to sniff out unexamined presuppositions, himself heavily presupposed the subjective side: that the mass of proletarians brought into being by the industrial revolution represented all of humanity, that they had the strategic societal position needed to transform advanced societies, and that they were on the road to possessing the will and the capacity to do so. This subjective side—the active human force reacting, cohering, organizing itself, challenging the dominant social relations, gaining the strength and self-confidence to do so, and perceiving the possibilities and limits of its situation—was fully half of Marxist hope.[6]

The historical fact is that Marx moved on to describe the objective processes of capitalism without dwelling on how masses of people accustomed to generations of submission might develop the disposition to displace the society's rulers.[7] The half of Marxist hope that occupied the bulk of his attention was the anticipated historical evolution of capitalist society, both in its growing productive capacity, its inability to use that capacity to meet human needs, and the increasingly unmanageable chaos its production relations would generate. Nevertheless, Marxist hope lay in the possibility of the objective and the subjective coming together, not merely in the system collapsing but in the workers having the subjective need and capacity to rise up and take control of it in its growing chaos.

From Comte to Stalin, there have been other programs of progress, embodying a kind of false hope that lacked actors, or programs of subjects acting more or less irrespective of the ripeness of objective conditions.[8] Practical efforts to realize Marxism were sometimes divorced from their dependence on propitious conditions, and sometimes Marxist thinkers and actors fell into waiting on events and conditions, and used these as excuses for a political passivity that betrayed their once revolutionary commitments.[9]

The danger in asking about "reasons to hope" today is that it casts the question in overly objectivist terms, trends that may never offer reasons to act—conditions without subjects. On the contrary, we have seen Martin Luther King argue that waiting on the flow of time means . . . waiting, never finding sufficient reasons to act. He argued that "the time is always ripe to do right," and thus for putting humans and their needs at the center of the reasons to act. The theoretical conclusion is that thinking about social hope today demands looking at subjective forces and their dispositions and objective situations, as well as the possibilities they offer. Hope is found, yes, and it is created. If hope is in trouble today, it is because the subject has gone missing. The studies of Progress, cynicism, and the privatization of hope in the previous chapters may help explain why this has happened. In the remaining pages of this book I will speak about how we might create it anew.

Whose Point of View?

Sartre captures the difference between seeing a struggle from the point of view of the subject and seeing it objectively. He discusses the ways in which the instructor in a military school is able to describe all the courses of action available to both sides in a battle in order to conclude which are the best possible moves. But this analytical activity cannot capture the situation of a combatant, who is "a blind and passionate man, sometimes desperate, sometimes ready to seek death, who risks everything in order to destroy the adversary," and who is concerned with seizing advantages, deploying resources, and avoiding destruction.[10]

The active stance I have described as *hoping* may make use of all of the available analysis, but it operates with the radical difference of being engaged. This carries with it the obvious disadvantages of being pressured by events, flustered, and forced to operate under conditions of stress and scarcity, but with the clarifying effect of trying to bring about a specific goal. Napoleon famously said, to be quoted a century later by Lenin: "First you commit yourself, and then you see." The point of view of a combatant brings with it an understanding that is otherwise inaccessible. From this perspective, countertrends and reasons to hope are no less and no more than a preface to engagement— which breaks with the contemplative or analytical stance for the sake of the practical project of changing the world.

Hope, then, can only be grasped by entering into it. It is something we produce among ourselves, in acting. To be sure, there can be degrees of hope, starting with passive observation of a developing situation in which we want to see a certain outcome, followed by the kind of vicarious hope that comes from identifying with the actual actors, or even the partisanship that accompanies giving them material and moral support. These ways of sharing the actors' hope are no small things. But the heart of the matter is in the action itself, including all the steps in organizing for it, and in keeping alive the organization that will carry out the action.

Hope is always self-created, beyond all possible reasons. Of course it helps to cite what we have accomplished in the past, and to describe the reasons why we can succeed in the present. And we may be inspired by those who act elsewhere.

But none of that is hope, and in a sense it is always beside the point. Hope lies in the active impulse of what we are doing together, here and now.

Hope amid Disaster

This means, paradoxically, that hope is sometimes built on the edge of despair, by people who are discouraged, angry, and humiliated, and who feel that they can no longer abide the treatment they are receiving or the impossible situation they are in. Sartre is helpful again: he describes the residents of the Quartier Saint-Antoine, in order to protect themselves against the king's troops, organizing themselves to take the Bastille, neutralize its cannon, and distribute its weapons among themselves. It was dire necessity that led to the rupture with their passive seriality and the creation of the collective activity of a group-in-fusion.[11]

Taking the Bastille was probably difficult for the residents to imagine, just as it always difficult to predict any coming together into a larger sense of solidarity and vision. Yet comings together occur again and again at times of natural and human-created catastrophe, as Rebecca Solnit describes with great power.[12] These are times when ordinary institutions collapse or lose their ability to cope with chaos and massive destruction. Solnit describes several historic moments in the United States, Canada, and Mexico when catastrophic events provoked spontaneously organized collective responses. These include the 1906 earthquake and fires in San Francisco, the Halifax munitions cargo ship explosion of 1917, the Mexico City earthquake of 1985, the events of 9/11, and Hurricane Katrina.

In such "paradises built from hell," people who normally live their lives at half-speed, trapped in stultifying and isolating socially imposed roles, rise to the occasion, organizing democratically and collectively to meet the community's urgent needs. "Two things matter about these ephemeral moments. First, they demonstrate what is possible or, perhaps more accurately, latent: the resilience and generosity of those around us and their ability to improvise another kind of society. Second, they demonstrate how deeply most of us desire connection, participation, altruism, and purpose."[13] Solnit is describing those utopian moments of hope, few and far between, when catastrophes lead to the breaking down of normal order, and demand that people collectively take control of their lives. Crises call on us to be flexible and improvisational, to treat each other as equals, and to take on meaningful roles in contributing to collective survival.

The lesson to draw from Solnit and Sartre is about hope arising as a collective response, in extremis, against danger and disaster, sorrow and suffering. In such times, hope can be an existential force, a drive for survival. From within the danger and the coming together, it is clear that hopeful action cannot be predicted, any more than the events of 1968, 1989, or 2011 could have been predicted. Someone, many someones, decided to act, usually after discussion and planning, and for some reason the impulse to act spread and took hold. It does not matter how many defeats have been suffered before the coming together, or what the odds are against it.

What is becoming clearer by the day is that we are now on the verge of such a galvanizing danger. We face the threat of a civilizational collapse (described by Diamond), or of environmental catastrophes foisted on the poor and walled off by the rich (described by Klein), or of "the disappearance of thousands of plant and animal species which we will never know, which our children will never see, because they have been lost forever" (described by Pope Francis). However normal and unchangeable our way of life and relations of power may seem today, however cynical and privatized the great majority of individuals in advanced societies may have become, another possibility remains latent in everyone. Once people come together to ward off the danger, the latent hope becomes activated, and there is no telling what they can or can't do. Is it only on this dubious and shaky terrain that hope will be created in the future?

Of course I am not speaking realistically. But were the Montgomery bus boycotters or the SNCC workers in Mississippi or the Selma marchers being realistic? The anti-nuclear demonstrators in New York City, in June 1983? Pope Francis, in relation to the entrenched church hierarchy as he embraced environmentalism and liberation theology? Jeremy Corbyn, when he decided to run for leader of the Labour Party? Bernie Sanders when he decided to run for president? And on the other hand, debate will go on for years about whether Syriza was being mistakenly realistic in capitulating to the European Troika after winning a massive majority against doing so. But what is beyond debate is that the hope we have been talking about has created new realities that did not exist before, such as a post-apartheid South Africa, the United Automobile Workers representing General Motors employees, the legitimacy of gay marriage. All these movements were most decidedly unrealistic in refusing to go along with the situations they were in. Yes, they did embrace realism in battle, about the lay of the land

and the balance of forces, but who could tell in advance what was possible, or what would happen?

Lessons of Hope

Listening to a young German friend talk about his community gardening project on Detroit's East Side in 2015 and again in 2016, as a veteran of community organizing in a Northern ghetto fifty years earlier, I could not help thinking how pathetic were today's efforts and how little progress they reflected. In 1965 white students and black residents of New Brunswick, New Jersey, had been stirred by the civil rights movement, the march from Selma to Montgomery, the riots in Watts, Harlem, and Newark, and the energies of Students for a Democratic Society projects in Newark and Hoboken. Those projects were explicitly political, aiming at the rats and roaches in people's apartments and at the system that allowed them. Today's Detroit garden project was part of no national movement, was not political, and took place in a depopulated city infamous for neglect and poverty. Its goal was to create a brief experience of community on the part of a dozen German and other students and, at best, a few dozen residents of the decaying neighborhood. Realistically speaking, what was accomplished? A few African Americans and mostly foreign students learned something about urban gardening. A few overcame racial barriers or uneasiness toward foreigners. A few on each side even developed a sense of community that overrode their usual individual self-centeredness. No movement was created or joined, no sparks of hope ignited and spread beyond the neighborhood. Yet the organizers felt enthusiastic because the projects actually came off without any disasters, good relations developed on all sides, and what they were trying to do met some success. Some lessons were learned, and one or two lives may have changed. Perhaps some people will look forward to the next similar project, or act differently, or take leadership of future community efforts.

By this effort my German friend taught me a great deal about hope. The project generated few conversations among the participants, between them and members of the community, or about the state of the world. Of course, constraints were built in: the project depended on a foundation grant and on the support of Jewish community organizations, and both the young people recruited to work there and the residents of the neighborhood had in mind a specific set of goals, which did not include challenging the social, political, and economic system. Thus, politics was ruled out from the start. This very political German friend was frustrated about the fact that politics did not crop up spontaneously in the interactions, but he accepted the limits built into the project and its specific goals of creating a self-sustaining community. Yet he never felt that it was worthless or insignificant. He insisted that no one knew what the results might be. The project was clearly worth doing for its own sake, and for the sake of the sense of community it generated, however fragile and limited that sense may have been. He taught me to respect this effort and to think as broadly as possible about the situation we are all in and the possible ways of reaching beyond it.

But the limits of the urban gardening project and its results lead me to wonder what I might be able to teach him about hope as I near the end of this book about hope in trouble, which has been a lifetime in the making. First, it is true that any social hope is all of hope[14]—not explicitly or consciously, but in its power to evoke hopes beyond itself that reach in every direction. A penumbra surrounds each act of social hope. Saving the rhinos, for example, implies protecting nature. Protecting nature implies protecting the commons. Saving animals and protecting the commons implies protecting other human beings. Merely organizing and acting to save the rhinos, attempting to change their current endangerment, empowers us with the sense that we can make a difference and change the destructive direction in which the world is heading. And it demands that we develop appropriate strengths and skills. The success of such acts is determined by the forces we can mobilize and the way we meet the opposition, and our understanding of those conditions will become crucial.

Second, I would pose a question: How can both urban gardening and saving the rhinos break out of the self-congratulatory and system-sustaining circle of doing good in the midst of the maelstrom in which we are all trapped? A popular movement goal is to "connect the dots." We have seen Pope Francis do that in "On Care for Our Common Home." How can it happen among urban gardeners and rhino savers?

Those who lament the narrowness of such efforts, as well as of today's identity politics, forget that many such specific causes—the community organizing project of fifty years ago, for example—once emerged within a much wider movement at a time of hope for fundamental change. As the broad movement receded, individual causes came to follow their own specific logics rather than supporting and seeking support from each other. A popular slogan in the 1960s was "One struggle, many fronts." No one knew exactly what this meant programmatically, but movement activists shared the deep sense that different oppressions—and oppressors—supported each other and were connected.

In those days it seemed obvious that each of the different currents of the wider movement needed to reach beyond themselves for understanding and encouragement, as well as to attack the general climate supporting various kinds of economic, political, social, and cultural oppression. Earlier in this book I mentioned poet Marge Piercy's 1969 dedication of *Hard Loving*, "from the Movement, for the Movement." At the time, everyone knew who she meant by "the Movement." Soon afterward, the Movement collapsed into fragments. For those who remained political, it was necessary to choose which fragment to belong to. And ever since, not simply former activists but the generations that followed, have had to act, live, and think among these bits and pieces. As unity became a memory, so did each specific movement's generous and dependent impulses.

My point is about the need to connect the dots between saving the rhinos and urban gardening—or, as Pope Francis has done, between capitalism, progress, inequality, and the destruction of the ecosystem. To reach out widely is to develop the habit of connecting the dots. Many people have responded to the ideas in this book by asking how I can insist that the hope I'm talking about has a specific political coloration. Why is social hope a particularly left-wing disposition? After all, don't others experience the kinds of hope I speak of? My answer so far has been that a specific sense of empowerment, democratic participation, equality, and generosity is what the left and no one else has been about. A second answer is that the determination to connect the dots between different kinds of suffering and social structures is equally a disposition of the left.

At the Detroit Zoo, I argued, participants in an urban gardening project would be able to visit the rhino exhibit, home to two endangered white rhinos. One natural result of such a visit might be a conversation about why these magnificent animals are endangered, why it matters that they survive, and what can be done to protect them. Another natural result might be a conversation about the zoo as a public place, what it means to us, and how it is able to survive. What all this has to do with urban gardening in Detroit is not immediately apparent, and that is just the point. People might make their own connections, but some of the connections might very well be subversive.[15]

Songs of Hope

This is not unlike making connections between gays and lesbians and striking miners. That effort to connect the dots is the story told in the 2014 movie *Pride*, which deals with gay and lesbian support for the UK miners' strike of 1983–84. It is captured in a song that occurs at a climactic moment in the film, when the striking men are on the defensive and are reluctant to accept the offer of gay and lesbian support. The leader of the young gay activists dramatically jumps on a table and pledges full and militant support and a spectacular action to come. After he shouts, "Victory to the miners," we hear from somewhere in the hall a beautiful female voice singing a cappella: "As we come marching, marching. . . ."

The song, "Bread and Roses," originated as a poem in 1911 and was first associated with the Lawrence textile workers strike the next year that was supported by the IWW and largely led by women. Since then, it has traditionally been sung as both

a women's movement and a labor song, and it was widely re-
corded after taking on its current musical form in the 1970s.
Its lyrics are quite specifically about women, beginning and
ending with:

> As we go marching, marching, in the beauty of the day
> A million darkened kitchens, a thousand mill lofts gray
> Are touched with all the radiance that a sudden sun discloses
> For the people hear us singing, bread and roses, bread and
> roses.
>
> * * *
>
> As we go marching, marching, we're standing proud and tall.
> The rising of the women means the rising of us all.
> No more the drudge and idler, ten that toil where one reposes,
> But a sharing of life's glories, bread and roses, bread and roses.

The music and lyrics reach from women to men, from
hunger to beauty, and then ultimately to everyone. This reach
toward a universal vision of liberation is captured and even
extended in the film, as the hall becomes hushed and people
listen to the woman singing. She rises after the first stanza,
and slowly, one after another, women stand and join her. Then
an instrumental accompaniment begins, the other people in
the hall stand, and even those who were initially hostile to the
gays and lesbians now join in song.

This musical moment does the several things that movement music has always done: it creates a sense of *we* acting
together for a just cause. In singing, people come to feel the
sense of belonging, solidarity, and even love that binds a move-

ment together, and they experience themselves reaching wide, possibly to all of humanity. The music stirs the emotions and inspires hope and strength as people collectively imagine that the world might be free and equal, peaceful, cooperative and caring, and that they are struggling together to bring this about. In singing, the members of the group experience key elements of hope: a sense of belonging to a much larger force than those in the room, of taking action and doing the right thing, of sharing this collective experience with each other, of feeling their potential power, of joining the great cause of all such movements, past and present. Other similar movement songs reaching back in time and around the world have included "The Internationale," "We Shall Overcome," "Give Peace a Chance," "Solidarity Forever," and "N'Kosi Sikalel Iafrica."

In *Pride*, singing the anthem conveys the radical intent of the film: one movement joins another, gays and lesbians join the miners, thereby implying that their causes and goals are ultimately the same. In the long run the hopes of the one entail the hopes of the other, and together something new comes into being. It is for the audience to think about how and why this is.[16]

We experience one further meaning of movement music when we sing one of the great anthems. It offers the possibility of dissolving the knot of futility that lodges itself in the throat of anyone who labors in the vain hope "that things will one day finally get better." What, after all, does the life experience of someone who hopes in the ways I have described amount to? Someone, say, who began in the New Left and many years on in an activist life, again and again tries to return to a sense of hope despite again and again experiencing setbacks and terrible new problems to struggle against, even in the face of victories. Is such a life ultimately futile? What can I tell my German friend, or my contemporaries? What can I tell myself?

A simple though not untroubled answer comes from a young, politically minded scholar whose work I've been encouraging during the last few years. In conversation about my looming sense of futility, she focuses not on what any of us is able to accomplish in a lifetime of struggle, which after all has not been able to protect the earth or our loved ones. We have not even been able in a molecular way to increase the chance that the next generation will be able to breathe easily. But more realistically, every last individual struggling for a better world can still point to two positive facts that are reflected when we sing together: others are bound to keep on, and despite all failures we at least have been able to encourage, inspire, or nourish some of those people.

Today, of course, even the best-lived life meets futility in its efforts to create a secure world; it is impossible to rest easy. But at the very least we know that the future remains open, that innumerable batons are still being picked up and carried forward, and that even after each of us is gone, we will not quit.

Postscript:
The New Politics of Hope

The year 2016 was a year like no other in American politics. It began amid widespread anticipation of a breakthrough: that the Democratic Party would nominate, and Americans would elect, a woman president. But as the primary season wore on, campaigns sprang up around individuals who were clearly outside the organizational, media, and fundraising mainstreams of US politics. In campaigning for the nominations of parties to which they had no significant ties, history, or loyalties, both men disdained courting party donors: Donald Trump financing his primary campaign with his own money, Bernie Sanders drawing millions of small donations. And both men made biting attacks on the party establishments. Holding mass rallies of thousands of supporters, each man created new organizational networks with roots in recent movements—the Tea Party in one case, Occupy in the other. Setting out against formidable odds, Trump facing a parade of establishment candidates, Sanders virtually ignored by the media, each man found ways to appeal to, and became buoyed by, millions who previously had been ignored by the political process. And so Trump won the nomination easily, while Sanders came surprisingly close and spooked Clinton and her supporters. Sanders "progressives" crystallized as a major force within the Democratic Party, and simultaneously as a movement to its left, but by the end of the year this remarkable development was virtually forgotten in the face of Donald Trump's startling victory. In the era described in this book, what do these two stunning insurgencies tell us about reviving social hope?

Obviously, both campaigns were responses to the troubled times many Americans had been experiencing for a decade, even a generation: the Great Recession and the twin nostrums of austerity and further privatization, as well as rising inequality, global terrorism, the loss of well-paying manufacturing employment to globalization, and declining working-class incomes and social power. This is all widely understood. What is not as widely understood is that the Sanders and Trump campaigns both rejected the conditions described earlier in this book: the individualized society, much of its cynicism, and the sense of living in an uncontrollable maelstrom which its people had been brought up to accept.

The Sanders and Trump campaigns both flew in the face of what I have discussed as the desocialization of social pain. Both rejected the privatizing of social expectations and the trend to marketize every possible aspect of social life. The secret of both insurgencies is the tenacity of social belonging in a neoliberal age. The fact is that Thatcher was wrong, the soul could not be changed; society could not be dissolved into its individuals. The 2016 election season strikingly demonstrated that social individuals would continue to resist their conversion into atoms, and would demand political solutions for political problems. Whether they will do so confusedly or clearly, as a mob or as a movement, destructively or constructively, the repressed has returned and will have its way.

The Sanders campaign sounded the most common themes of past progressive movements in the democratic tradition of the Enlightenment, and it gave political shape to the most recent of these, Occupy and the climate change movement. From the living wage to student debt, from the climate crisis to the rise in inequality, from universal health care to control of the political system by the very rich, the campaign responded explicitly to the issues with a sense of idealism, universalism, and solidarity. In a society with a sorry history of such movements in national electoral politics, at first there was little reason to believe that the Sanders campaign would be more than the usual protest candidacy at the margins of a presidential race. But Sanders continued to gain support, organizers, and funding; and his dramatic rallies, which drew young people in the thousands, let everyone know that something new was happening as the seemingly quixotic campaign very quickly became a mass movement.

The campaign's byword of "revolution" showed Sanders's perception that the time was right to think not only of protest but of gaining political control from the very wealthy and bringing about significant change. Calling himself a "democratic socialist" flouted an equally great taboo in American politics, also without penalty, and it linked him with a tradition even earlier than the 1960s, whose deep history was further suggested by his age, bearing, and white hair. By so doing, Sanders proudly situated himself within the historical moral climate I described in chapter 2, the cumulative result of struggles for justice, peace, and freedom. "Socialism" had seemed to be a dead and buried part of that climate, and the very vagueness of Sanders's statements about it turned out to be a strength, giving listeners the capacity to imagine alternative possibilities to the system they were more and more coming to oppose.[1]

To be sure, Barack Obama had conjured a sense of hope in 2008 that both reflected his deepest convictions and spoke to a strongly felt need among his supporters. Hope was one of Obama's main ideas: "having the audacity to believe despite all the evidence to the contrary that we could restore a sense of community to a nation torn by conflict; the gall to believe that despite personal setbacks, the loss of a job or an illness in the family or a childhood mired in poverty, we had some control—and therefore responsibility—over our own fate."[2] And he clearly understood the connection between hope and action, his stirring speeches in 2008 reflecting a keen sense of the difficulty of hope. Obama's "hope" became an inspiring campaign slogan, resting in the end on his supporters' newness to politics as well as the newness of this previously unknown political figure who not so incidentally would be the first African American president. But operationally, Obama's "hope" became narrowed to asking his supporters to get him elected. The Sanders campaign, on the other hand, neither rested on a concept of hope nor marketed "hope" as a watchword; it became a movement. Actually embodying social hope, it not only created a sense of collectivity but brought with it other traits of movements discussed in chapter 2 of this book, such as their universalist values, their will to create change, and their sense of potency. The Sanders campaign focused on relations of power and privilege, and talked about changing a system of inequality and poverty. Thus it generated a concrete sense of possibility, based on the from-the-ground-up fact that it raised its own money from millions of small donors. Not beholden to large contributors or to the campaign finance system, the Sanders campaign carried with it a sense of purpose and integrity rarely seen in US politics.

Sincerity, idealism, an absence of cynicism, and a sense of possibility—the stuff of hope—were among the Sanders movement's most visible attributes, which contrasted strikingly with most other American politics, including the Clinton campaign. Except for the "democratic socialist" label and the "revolution" theme, Sanders avoided voicing general appeals, and instead hammered away at several specific proposals. Although most of these proposals amounted to enlarging the American welfare state in a Scandinavian direction, they did so by embracing and regulating the existing capitalist system, except for calling for breakup of the big banks. But the general appeal was implicit in the specific proposals: to reduce inequality by insisting that the very rich pay a "fair share" of their income in taxes, to mandate a living wage and government-funded universal health care, to end the system of campaign financing and thus make elections more democratic, to provide universal opportunity for free college education, to end the sway of corporate-friendly "free trade" agreements, and to protect the environment. The appeal was thus not at all for socialism in the sense of worker control or an end to capitalism, but for a political reversal of the oligarchic direction of American society.

The social-democratic acceptance of capitalism contained a clear insistence on government intervention on behalf of workers, the environment, and citizens, and a clear reversal of the privatization of the social that had been taking place over the past generation. The socialism of the Sanders movement was above all a determination to think and act socially and to tackle collective problems collectively. Where the new sense of solidarity and activist intervention would lead was anybody's guess, except that it was a clear reversal of the trends of American life since the 1970s, an uprising against the prevailing cynicism, individualism, and passivity toward the maelstrom that was shaping people's lives.

Following from Occupy, similar to Podemos and Syriza, and simultaneous with Jeremy Corbyn's ascendancy in the Labour Party, the Sanders campaign flew in the face of what was widely accepted as realistic, and in the process it redefined reality. Each of these movements embodied a strong sense of alternative possibility. In bringing isolated individuals together in action, they revived social hope.

And Donald Trump? Like the Sanders movement, Trump reflected the growing awareness that something fundamental was wrong in American society, and that the political system had become incapable of responding effectively and was indeed part of the problem. Trump too attracted millions of supporters by voicing genuine grievances—particularly, as Thomas Frank pointed out, about the destructive effects of transnational pacts such as the North American Free Trade Agreement (NAFTA). His core supporters lived in "the zones of economic misery that 30 years of Washington's free-market consensus have brought the rest of America."[3] Like Sanders, Trump mobilized people who were furious at the elites and structures of his party—people who were angry at "the system." He, too, rejected the customary dependency on fundraising, going even further than Sanders by using his own monetary wealth to avoid the problem altogether and brilliantly manipulating the media into providing endless free coverage.

Mobilizing many of the activists, organizations, and energies that had made the Tea Party a major force in the Republican Party since 2009, Trump defeated a parade of establishment candidates. Under the slogan "Make America great again," he attracted millions of followers with his entertaining free-form rants against the establishment and his shameless self-promotion. The Sanders movement was in its own way motivated by anger—at the cost of health care and college, the increase in inequality, the political power of the 1 percent, the campaign finance system, the corporations that move jobs overseas, and the fact that millions of workers do not make a living wage.

It took the rest of the country many months to realize that many of Trump's supporters were thoughtful participants who had reasons for resonating with his message. As Alexander Zaitchik described it, they were not taken in by him and they listened skeptically to such proposals as building a wall with Mexico and rounding up illegal immigrants; sometimes they were even troubled about his instability. But what attracted them was that Trump spoke more seriously than his Republican opponents or Hillary Clinton about what troubled them most: the loss of manufacturing and mining jobs, the poor treatment of military veterans, and the movement of drugs and criminals across the border with Mexico. Arlie Hochschild makes clear that part of Trump's message dovetailed with years of right-wing attacks on a government that, to many whites, seemed indifferent to their welfare while being devoted to advancing minorities, welcoming immigrants, and encouraging jobs to leave the country. Trump's trash-talking and stance as a businessman drew people to him who had become fed up with the empty reassurances of politicians for whom free-market globalization was the governing creed and deindustrialization was virtually ignored. Trump was seen as someone who spoke the truth and was determined to do something for those who had become invisible to the politicians.[4]

At the same time, those who voted for Trump gave implicit consent to his bigotry; some even supported it openly. Trump's victorious campaign was a weird distorting-mirror inversion of the Sanders movement, built not on generosity but on fear, racism, authoritarianism, nostalgia, and a profound cynicism. It contradicted the essential features of social hope described in this book: collective action of a *we* committed to forging, expanding, and deepening democracy. As we have seen, some key descriptive terms of such an active *we* devoted to creating a more just world have included universality, collective action, and its participants' sense of capability, possibility, and solidarity. Social hope draws from and adds to a moral climate that has historically inspired and contributed to movements around the world. In contrast, the Trump campaign was an anti-hope current, and in fact was defensive and exclusivist. Although its supporters shared a collective sensibility, that sensibility was an angry wallowing in nostalgia that never reached out to the rest of humanity.

If the Bernie Sanders campaign represented a revival of social hope, "Trumpism" became *the* anti-hope. Trump made himself into a spokesperson for a significant remnant of the white working class, appealing to those who lived on in the deindustrialized landscape, strangers in a society whose current vitality had become postindustrial, global, multiracial, and multicultural. "Trumpism" came to mean aggrieved white men who looked toward the past and were angry about free trade, who were hostile to immigrants and minorities but not (heaven forbid!) to the capitalist system, who were mobilized against terrorists but not overly concerned about madmen armed with assault rifles—and who lacked any progressive vision of the future or of any action they themselves might take other than gathering around a narcissistic con man and cheering his outrageous rants. And, of course, voting for him. As Rick Perlstein has said, the Trump campaign seemed to reprise an American tradition: Trump as the snake oil salesman and his supporters as his marks.[5] Moreover, for all the energy it generated, the Trump campaign never quite became a movement. In this sense it was anti-hope in form as well as substance. As Brian Beutler argued, Trump was not "a typical movement leader." Movement leaders "sometimes achieve measures of fame, but much of the work of movement-building is done in the field, and requires strategic acumen, organizing, fundraising, mobilization, recruitment, endurance, and ideological dedication."[6] Very little of this happened during the Trump campaign, and very little was asked of his followers. Yes, Trump supporters turned out at rallies, followed his Twitter comments, and voted for him. But unlike the Sanders insurgency, the Trump campaign was not at all about what *we* might do, but what *he* would do. Indeed, the Trump phenomenon was unique in revolving around the personality of its leader. Since Trump's main campaign pitch was to sell his ability as a fixer and a deal-maker to solve the country's problems, it is unsurprising that his core supporters scored well beyond those of all other Republicans on one scholar's scale of authoritarianism.[7]

The great businessman preening himself in public had not been produced by a political party, labor unions, civic groups, or community organizations. He was not a leader of grass-roots activism seeking to create a different future in concrete ways. Instead of envisioning a new kind of common good or celebrating universal values, many of Trump's supporters nurtured, in sometimes overtly hateful and sometimes hidden "dog-whistle" ways, what was left of their dignity—their whiteness. Indeed, one survey carried out during the primary season revealed their negative attitude toward every social group except themselves and the police.[8]

Trump's voters longed for change. They wanted, after all, to "shake things up," but in what direction? Specifically what "things"? And specifically how? Such vagueness suggests that many of his supporters hungered for brash, cynical posturing—not bullshit exactly, but obscene gestures to "the system" and all those whom they perceived to be bothering them. Shaking up the system, giving it the finger: these things were the opposite of Sanders's "political revolution." And of course, by electing the snake oil salesman, they brought into power with him another, darker side of the same system. The anti-hope of Donald Trump is an old and familiar story but also a frighteningly current one, from Italian fascism and Nazism to Brexit, France's National Front, Austria's Freedom Party, and the Dutch Party for Freedom. Animated not by social hope but by ethnic, economic, cultural, and racial defensiveness, people still hope, but they do so in narrowly construed, nostalgic, and sometimes vicious ways. They raise authoritarian leaders and may develop murderous force—but their anti-other hope is a contradiction in terms that is rooted ultimately in despair about taking positive collective action.

The anti-hope movements, appearing around the world at the same time, may continue to flourish, or they may be defeated or die out. The new movements for social hope around the world may retreat, be defeated, peter out, or give rise to strategies and institutional and cultural structures that are capable of nourishing them over the long term. Perhaps then, things will finally get better and all "humans will one day be allowed to breathe easily"? How things turn out will depend on what we do.

Notes

A Note on We

1. Eugene Zamiatin (Evgeny Zamyatin), *We* (New York, 1959), 13.
2. Ibid., 6–7.

Chapter 1

1. And even where he talked about it, at the beginning of "Progress," its use is not unambiguous. Adorno only says that the concept of progress "promises: an answer to the doubt and the hope that things will finally get better. . . ." But employing the concept dogmatically "cheats" us out of being able to answer the question. Theodore Adorno, "Progress," in Gary Smith, ed., *Benjamin: Philosophy, Aesthetics, History* (Chicago, 1990), 84.
2. Stephen Pinker, *The Better Angels of Our Nature: Why Violence Has Declined* (New York, 2011).
3. Iris Young, *Justice and the Politics of Difference* (Princeton, 1990).
4. See François Furet, *The Passing of an Illusion: The Idea of Communism in the Twentieth Century* (Chicago, 1999); and Ronald Aronson, "Communism's Posthumous Trial," *History and Theory* 42 (May 2003).
5. Meaghan Morris, *The Pirate's Fiancée: Feminism, Reading, Postmodernism* (London, 1988), 53.
6. See Ronald Aronson, *After Marxism* (New York, 1995), 168–79.

7. See *After Marxism*, 276–82; and Ronald Aronson, *Living without God* (Berkeley, 2008), chapter 7.

8. Jean-François Lyotard, "Universal History and Cultural Differences," in *The Lyotard Reader*, ed. Andrew Benjamin (Oxford, 1989), 316.

9. Wendy Brown, *Undoing the Demos: Neoliberalism's Stealth Revolution* (New York, 2015), 17.

10. Brown's analysis is a major contribution to our efforts to understand our present situation. While agreeing with much of it, this book takes a somewhat different direction. I am concerned with the withering of social hope today from the standpoint of past and potential social movements. My topic is the *absence* of movement, which is to say the withering of social hope. In searching for causes, I will dwell on the maelstrom of Progress resulting from the absence of any sense of collective agency, the cynicism of isolated individuals generated by consumer society, and the privatization of hopes that once were social. Brown's concern for the neoliberal economization of society and people is vital to my analysis, but my focus is the accompanying desocialization and individualization. At the same time, I will stress the deep reserves of social identity latent in all of us, and the fact that recent individualizing identity changes are in a deep sense unnatural. I look for today's sources of desocialization from a standpoint that anticipates ways in which the left can recreate itself and resume its projects.

11. Jürgen Habermas, *Theory of Communicative Action, Vol 1: Reason and the Rationalization of Society* (Boston, 1984); *Theory of Communicative Action, Vol 2: Lifeworld and System: A Critique of Functionalist Reason*, Boston, 1987); Michel Foucault, *The Birth of Biopolitics: Lectures at the College de France 1978-79* (New York, 2010).

12. Wendy Brown, "Booked #3: What Exactly Is Neoliberalism?" Interview with Timothy Shenk, *Dissent*, April 2, 2015; https://www.dissent magazine.org/blog/booked-3-what-exactly-is-neoliberalism-wendy -brown-undoing-the-demos.

13. Eric Hobsbawm, *The Age of Revolution 1789–1848* (New York, 1964), 287.

14. David Caute, *The Left in Europe since 1789* (New York, 1966).

15. Geoff Eley, *Forging Democracy: The History of the Left in Europe 1850–2000* (New York, 2002).

16. In fact, two of the campaign's major hopes were achieved. One, the historic breakthrough of an African American becoming president, was indeed something "we" achieved, but it was quickly forgotten by many of his original supporters. The other, national health insurance, was a major collective goal that was passed only with individual responsibility and corporate profit at its center.

17. Francis Fukuyama, *The End of History and the Last Man* (New York, 1992), 46.

18. See Perry Anderson, *A Zone of Engagement* (London, 1992), and Robert Heilbroner, *A Vision of the Future* (New York, 1995).

19. Of course serious social planning will also make use of market incentives. Some thinkers have been studying ways to mitigate climate change by putting a price on carbon emissions. The claim is that prices can induce separate, uncoordinated individuals toward a similar goal, even if they haven't deliberately organized. The evidence in favor of this plan includes the fact that rising gas prices are correlated with buying more efficient cars, and the fact that better wages attract workers.

Chapter 2

1. The work that tries to convey and comprehend all of these is Ernst Bloch's *The Principle of Hope* (Cambridge, MA, 1986). See my analysis in *After Marxism* (New York, 1995), chapter 11.

2. Terry Eagleton, *Hope without Optimism* (London, 2015), 114.

3. See Ronald Aronson, *The Dialectics of Disaster: A Preface to Hope* (London, 1984).

4. Patrick Shade, *Habits of Hope: A Pragmatic Theory* (Nashville, 2001), 70.

5. Jean-Paul Sartre, *Critique of Dialectical Reason* (London, 1976), 253–404.

6. Rebecca Solnit, *Hope in the Dark: Untold Histories, Wild Possibilities* (Chicago, 2016), xii.

7. Ibid., 5.

8. Solnit, 109.

9. This is how Geoff Eley describes the history of the European left in *Forging Democracy*.

10. One of the key features of cynicism is that it drastically shrinks the

region of what appears to be realistic—to the existing situation. More on this in chapter 4.

11. Martin Murray, *Democracy Deferred: The Painful Birth of Post-Apartheid South Africa* (London, 1994).

12. For a comparison of the US civil rights movement with the Israeli-Palestinian struggle, see Ronald Aronson, "*Selma* and the Israeli-Palestinian Struggle," *Humanistic Judaism* 18 (2015), no. 1.

13. Steve Golin, *The Fragile Bridge* (Philadelphia, 1989), 137.

14. Sidney Fine, *Sit-Down* (Ann Arbor, 1968), 158.

15. Ibid., 199.

16. Ibid., 157.

17. Genora Johnson Dollinger, interview, September 22, 1978, University of Michigan–Flint, http://www.umflint.edu/archives/genora-johnson-dollinger.

18. Fine, 267.

19. Dollinger, interview.

20. Fine, 331.

21. Barack Obama, *The Audacity of Hope: Thoughts on Reclaiming the American Dream* (New York, 2006).

22. Martin Luther King, Jr., Speech to MIA Mass Meeting at Holt Street Baptist Church, December 5, 1955, https://kinginstitute.stanford.edu/king-papers/documents/mia-mass-meeting-holt-street-baptist-church.

23. Isaac Deutscher, *The Prophet Armed: Trotsky 1879–1921* (London, 2004); see chapter 14.

24. In fact, by the late 1980s the ANC and the South African state had arrived at a stalemate, which was to be broken only by the end of the Cold War, and by changes set off by the negotiated withdrawal of Cuban troops from Angola and the South African withdrawal from Namibia. When F. W. de Klerk came to power and released Nelson Mandela from prison, the situation changed.

Chapter 3

1. President Jimmy Carter defied this with his "crisis of confidence" speech, and lost the next election to Ronald Reagan, for whom it was "morning in America." See note 23.

2. Sophocles: *Fragments*, Volume 3 (Cambridge, MA, 2003), fragment 948, 409.

3. There it runs from the first Christians' fervent anticipations of Christ's second coming and the judgment day to St. Paul's "faith, hope, and charity," and to Augustine's *Enchiridion on Faith, Hope, and Love* and his "hope of happiness" in the afterlife in the *City of God*. It is famously defined with Aristotelian clarity by St. Thomas Aquinas as "a movement of appetite aroused by the perception of what is agreeable, future, arduous, and possible of attainment." Cited by Brian Davies, *Thomas Aquinas's "Summa Theologiae": A Guide and Commentary* (Oxford, 2014), 184.

4. Nicolas de Caritat, Marquis de Condorcet, *Sketch for a Historical Picture of the Progress of the Human Mind*. The Tenth Stage – The Future Progress of the Human Mind (New York, 1955), 173.

5. Ibid., 179.

6. Condorcet was committed to spreading Europe's "principles and example of . . . freedom, reason, and illumination" to the rest of the world, starting with Africa and Asia. Europe's passion to enlighten other peoples was offered ample scope and opportunity by the "vast lands" overseas. Some of the peoples of these countries were only waiting for Europeans to appear in order to learn from their example; others needed to be delivered from oppression. Still others, savages or conquering hordes, perhaps could not be helped. It was possible that this third group, unable to benefit from European progress and "reduced in number as they are driven back" by Europeans, would "finally disappear imperceptibly before them or merge into them." Ibid., 177. Thus did Condorcet's story of human progress, reflecting a very particular ideology, anticipate the elimination of a part of humanity.

7. See his brilliant and totally self-conscious early essay, "Plan of the Scientific Operations Necessary for Reorganizing Society," as well as the editor's illuminating essay in *August Comte and Positivism: The Essential Writings* (Chicago, 1975), ed. Gertrude Lenzer.

8. Thus, as Georges Sorel forcefully argued a century ago in *Les Illusions du progrès (The Illusion of Progress)*—and as Christopher Lasch later emphasized in the American context—exponents of Progress were not

simply describing the facts, but were arranging them. See Lasch, *The True and Only Heaven: Progress and Its Critics* (New York, 1991).

9. In the words of the director of the Columbian Exposition, "The best thought, the most advanced methods of all countries in science, literature, reform, education, government, morals, philanthropy, jurisprudence—indeed, all those things which contribute to the progress, prosperity, and peace of mankind—are exhibited in the Exposition itself, or discussed in its Auxiliary Congresses." Trumbull White and Wm. Igleheart, *The World's Columbian Exposition, Chicago, 1893: A Full Description of the Buildings and Exhibits in All Departments: And a Short Account of Previous Expositions with an Introduction / by Col. George R. Davis; and an Introduction to the Woman's Department by Mrs. Potter Palmer; with Special Chapters by Hon. Thomas B. Bryan, . . . [et al.]* (Philadelphia, 1893), 19, at https://archive.org/stream/worldscolumbiane00whit#page /n7/mode/2up.

10. Michael S. James, "1900's New Century Hype Was Millennial," *ABC News*, December 31, 2000, http://abcnews.go.com/US/1900s-century -hype-millennial/story?id=89978.

11. Karl Marx and Frederick Engels, *The Communist Manifesto* (London, 1998), 40–41.

12. Martin Luther King, Jr., "Letter from a Birmingham Jail," April 16, 1963, https://kinginstitute.stanford.edu/king-papers/documents/letter -birmingham-jail.

13. Ronald G. Havelock, "Acceleration," in *Acceleration: The Forces Driving Human Progress* (Amherst, NY, 2011).

14. See John Gray, *The Silence of Animals: On Progress and Other Myths* (New York, 2014), and *Heresies: Against Progress and other Illusions* (London, 2004).

15. Matt Ridley, *The Rational Optimist: How Prosperity Evolves* (New York, 2010); Charles Kenny, *Getting Better: Why Global Development is Succeeding—and How We Can Improve the World Even More* (New York, 2011).

16. Pinker, *The Better Angels of our Nature*, 693.

17. Ibid., 694; the claim on intelligence is on 658.

18. See note 9.

19. Marx and Engels, *Communist Manifesto*, 62.

20. Sidney Pollard, *The Idea of Progress: History and Society* (New York, 1972), 183.
21. Ibid.
22. Isaac Deutscher, *Stalin: A Political Biography* (Oxford, 1948), last chapter.
23. See David Graeber, "Of Flying Cars and the Declining Rate of Profit," *The Baffler* 19 (2012), http://thebaffler.com/salvos/of-flying-cars-and -the-declining-rate-of-profit; Owen Paepke, *The Evolution of Progress: The End of Economic Growth and the Beginning of Human Transformation* (New York, 1992).
24. See www.pbs.org/wgbh/americanexperience/features/primary-resources /carter-crisis/.
25. Heilbroner later brought a stronger ecological consciousness into a similar reflection that any "hopes for the very long-term prospects for humankind" meant reversing the trend of industrial civilization:

    > Humankind must achieve a secure terrestrial basis for life. The earth must be lovingly maintained, not consumed nor otherwise despoiled. The atmosphere, the waters, and the fertility of the soil must be protected against poisoning of any kind from human activities. The population of the globe must be stabilized at levels easily accommodated to the earth's carrying capacity under technological and social conditions that we—and presumably they— would find agreeable. Without such a stable foundation, there seems little chance to attain a level of civilization unmistakably more advanced than our own.

    Robert Heilbroner, *Visions of the Future* (New York, 1995), 115.
26. Ronald Wright, *A Short History of Progress* (New York, 2005); see also the film, by Wright, *Surviving Progress* (2011).
27. Why are they out of control? Diamond's concern in *Collapse: How Societies Choose to Fail or Succeed* (New York, 2005), drawn from the study of civilizations that failed, is the need for societies to change their "core values." The critic Richard Smith points out two difficulties with this analysis. First, by stressing attitudes, Diamond ignores the economic system that generates both today's problems and the attitudes that obscure them. Taking free-market capitalism as given, Diamond would try to alter the values of those who operate the system—as if the problems

are not rooted in structural priorities such as maximizing profits and economic growth. Second, when it comes to contemporary society, Diamond ignores his own analysis of civilizations that failed; he often talks not about "societies;" but about social classes with different interests, about rulers and ruled. One example is the competition among chiefs on Easter Island that totally ignored the well-being of their subjects and drove the society into irremediable decline. Smith's point is that the issues Diamond raises require massive action that goes against the essential structural interests of the system and those running it—for example, unless the corporation is challenged along with the economic system's imperative need for profits and growth, no national strategy to make and sell fewer cars is thinkable. Capitalism itself is today's "progress trap." Richard Smith, "The Engine of Eco Collapse: Jared Diamond Ignores His Own Lessons," *Climate & Capitalism*, February 14, 2007, http://climateandcapitalism.com/2007/02/14/the-engine-of-eco-collapse -jared-diamond-ignores-his-own-lessons/.

28. Herbert Marcuse, *One-Dimensional Man: Studies in the Ideology of Advanced Industrial Society* (Boston, 1964); see Ronald Aronson, "Marcuse Today," *Boston Review*, November 17, 2014; http://www.bostonreview .net/books-ideas/ronald-aronson-herbert-marcuse-one-dimensional -man-today.

29. Benjamin speaks sneeringly about social-democratic talk of progress in "Theses on the Philosophy of History," in *Illuminations* (New York, 1969).

30. Ibid, 257–58.

31. André Gorz, *Critique of Economic Reason* (London, 1988), 121. Habermas has something similar in mind when he talks about the "colonization of the lifeworld."

32. Marx and Engels, *Communist Manifesto*, 41.

33. Brown, 221.

34. Golin, 35.

35. John Dewey, "Progress," *International Journal of Ethics* (April 1916), 312.

36. Ibid., 315.

37. Ibid., 318.

38. Ibid., 315.

Chapter 4

1. William Chaloupka, *Everybody Knows: Cynicism in America* (Minneapolis, 2001), 5.

2. Andreas Huyssen, foreword to Peter Sloterdijk, *Critique of Cynical Reason* (Minneapolis, 1987), xi.

3. An example of someone devoting his energies to combating cynicism is E. J. Dionne, especially in *Why Americans Hate Politics* (New York, 1991).

4. This is discussed in Chaloupka, chapter 16.

5. Sharon Stanley, "Retreat from Politics: The Cynic in Modern Times," *Polity* 39.3 (July 2007): 389.

6. Harry Frankfort, *On Bullshit* (Princeton, NJ, 2005).

7. See Slavoj Žižek, *The Sublime Object of Ideology* (London, 2008); Mark Fisher, *Capitalist Realism* (Ropley, Hants, 2008).

8. Chaloupka, xiv.

9. Ibid., 14.

10. http://www.idea.int/publications/vt/upload/Voter%20turnout.pdf.

11. Stefan Lorenz Sorgner, "In Search of Lost Cheekiness: An Introduction to Peter Sloterdijk's 'Critique of Cynical Reason,'" http://www.tabvlarasa .de/20/sorgner.php.

12. Stanley, 386.

13. Ibid.

14. Žižek, 25–30 and 200.

15. Fisher.

16. Not the only soil. It also flourishes when one is condemned to mandatory participation in an externally dominated group whose slogans are the opposite of common experience, as in the old Soviet Union.

17. A note on realism: Of course reality must be acknowledged. Discouraged former activists of the left can easily point to their own failures to make any positive difference, and some among them may be discouraged by the outcomes of the twentieth century's revolutionary and reformist movements, or by its catastrophic wars, or by the negative effects of progress. In turn, many of today's activists and their supporters pride themselves on being realistic, and do so for good reason. Thousands of specific causes enroll millions of activists the world over. A random local list might call for a living wage, gun control, protection against rape,

lower university tuitions, bans of fracking, safeguards of the water supply, mortgage foreclosure relief, shelter for the homeless, protection of
a particular species of wildlife, control of police violence against minorities, increases in renewable energy, an end to this or that one of America's endless wars, and limits on sugared drinks, among many other
causes. Many of these movements are clearly focused and well organized, and will achieve results. But despite all the activism and the energy
that drives it, everyone knows that most of these problems have deeper
roots, are connected institutionally to certain interests, and continue to
remain untouched and undiscussed. Further, pathways for significant
reform are blocked, and the larger social movements that seek structural change have long since been exhausted. In a hundred years we
have gone from socialist movements claiming to solve every possible
problem in a single stroke to separate movements frozen in their separateness. The realism of these latter movements must be honored. But,
as Naomi Klein points out about many environmental organizations, a
realism that is unwilling to connect the dots can easily succumb to the
abuses it is trying to change. In a deeper sense than one imagines, it is
unrealistic not to seek the levers for changing the abuses at their source.

18. Kathleen Hall Jamieson and Joseph N. Cappella, *Cynicism: The Press and
the Public Good* (New York, 1997).

19. Adam Smith, *The Wealth of Nations* (New York, 1937), 14.

20. Free-market ideology celebrates the magic of today's market in a world
infinitely more complex than the one in which Smith lived. As Paul
Krugman points out day after day in the *New York Times*, free-market ideology makes little sense after the Great Depression, the consumer society
described in Galbraith's *The Affluent Society*, the Great Recession, etc.

21. Why does Marx refer ironically to Bentham, the philosopher of utili-
tarianism, and not to Adam Smith, the originator of the philosophy of
self-interest? The key may lie in Marx's hostility: he calls Bentham "an
arch-Philistine" and an "insipid, pedantic, leather-tongued oracle of the
ordinary bourgeois intelligence of the 19th century." In a footnote he
adds: "With the driest naivete he [Bentham] takes the modern shopkeeper, especially the English shopkeeper, as the normal man. Whatever

is useful to this queer normal man, and to his world, is absolutely useful. *This yard-measure, then, he applies to past, present, and future. . . .* [Bentham is] a genius in the way of bourgeois stupidity." Karl Marx, *Capital*, vol. 1 (London, 2010) (vol. 35 of Marx and Engels *Collected Works*), part 7, chapter 24, note 50, 605.

22. Ibid., part 2, chapter 6 ("The Buying and Selling of Labour-Power)," 186.
23. John K. Galbraith, *The Affluent Society* (New York, 1958), 158.
24. Guy Debord, *The Society of the Spectacle* (Detroit, 1983), 37.
25. Ibid., 38.
26. Robert Heilbroner, *Business Civilization in Decline* (New York, 1976), 113.
27. Phillipe Odou and Pauline de Pechpeyrou, "Consumer Cynicism: From Resistance to Anti-Consumption in a Disenchanted World?" *European Journal of Marketing* 45, no. 11/12 (2011).
28. Frankfort, 22.
29. Ibid., 55.
30. Ibid., 22.
31. Whether or not the "no" campaign in Chile in 1988 was cynical, *No*, Pablo Larrain's 2012 film about it, certainly was.
32. See http://www.motherjones.com/politics/2011/12/leadup-iraq-war -timeline.
33. See Jeffrey Goldfarb, *The Cynical Society* (Chicago, 1991), 51.

Chapter 5

1. Thomas B. Edsall, "Why Don't the Poor Rise Up?" *New York Times*, June 24, 2015. http://www.nytimes.com/2015/06/24/opinion/why-dont-the-poor -rise-up.html?_r=0.
2. "Polling the Tea Party," *New York Times*, April 14, 2010, http://www .nytimes.com/interactive/2010/04/14/us/politics/20100414-tea-party -poll-graphic.html.
3. Mark Lilla, "The Tea Party Jacobins," *New York Review of Books*, May 27, 2010, http://www.nybooks.com/articles/archives/2010/may/27/tea-party -jacobins/?pagination=false.

4. Rick Santelli. "We're thinking of having a Chicago Tea Party in July. All you capitalists that want to show up to Lake Michigan, I'm going to organize it." http:/www.thedailybeast.com/articles/2015/10/30/when-cnbc -created-the-tea-party.html.

5. Quoted in Anthony DiMaggio and Paul Street, "What Populist Uprising? Part 2: Further Reflections on an 'Astroturf Movement,'" http:// mrzine.monthlyreview.org/2010/ds290410.html.

6. See Will Bunch, *The Backlash: Right-Wing Radicals, High-Def Hucksters, and Paranoid Politics in the Age of Obama* (New York, 2010).

7. So much so that Anthony DiMaggio and Paul Street argue that, far from representing a genuine social movement, "the Tea Party is more accurately described as a top-down interest group led by national and local political officials and financed by corporate America." Granted, it has been unable to unite under a single organizational umbrella, its grassroots organizing seems weak to nonexistent, and a national Tea Party convention was canceled no less than three times. But use of the term "interest group" too quickly dismisses the hundreds of thousands of conservative activists energized after the Republicans' demoralizing defeat in 2008—including the more than two thousand who turned out at the Chicago rally that DiMaggio and Street describe. The disturbing reality is that the Tea Partiers—mass social movement or not, unified or not— have achieved a real political presence. As Vanessa Williamson, Theda Skocpol, and John Coggin conclude from their research in the Boston area, the Tea Party "energized disgruntled white middle-class conservatives," who form its activist base. As a result, "it has sapped Democratic momentum, revitalized Republican conservatism, and pulled the national Republican Party towards the far right." So far, these are more lasting achievements than the New Left managed during its entire life span.

8. Ulrich Beck, *The Risk Society: Towards a New Modernity* (London, 1992), 135.

9. Alexis de Tocqueville, *Democracy in America* (Books@Adelaide, 2014), book 2, chapter 2, "Of Individualism in Democratic Countries."

10. David Whitman, *The Optimism Gap* (New York, 1998), 13.

11. "In percentage terms, 41% are optimists about the nation's future, while 33% are pessimists. This compares starkly to 55% who are optimists about

their personal lives, while only 13% are pessimists. Historically, the gap between these two measures is at an all time high." "The Optimism Gap Grows," January 16, 1997, http://www.people-press.org/1997/01/17/the-optimism-gap-grows/.

12. See Jean Twenge, *Generation Me, Revised and Updated: Why Today's Young Americans Are More Confident, Assertive, Entitled—and More Miserable Than Ever Before* (New York, 2006); Jean M. Twenge and W. Keith Campbell, *The Narcissism Epidemic: Living in the Age of Entitlement* (New York, 2009); Eva S. Moskowitz, *In Therapy We Trust: America's Obsession with Self-Fulfillment* (Baltimore, 2001).

13. See Tony Judt, *Ill Fares the Land* (New York, 2010), 86–88. When Judt castigates the New Left for "the decline of a shared sense of purpose," one can only wonder where he was at the time. The same applies to Mark Lilla's discussion of the New Left in "The Tea Party Jacobins." See Staughton, Lynd, and Lilla, " 'The Tea Party Jacobins': An Exchange," *New York Review of Books,* August 19, 2010, http://www.nybooks.com/articles/archives/2010/aug/19/tea-party-jacobins-exchange/.

14. Judt does manage to capture this, and to correctly place it as one of the sources of the negative features of the more recent past.

15. Jessica Reynolds, "Relationship Annoyance: Deal Breaker or a Minor Quirk?" *Chicago Tribune* (TNS); this appeared in the *Detroit Free Press,* July 20, 2015, 1C.

16. Barbara Ehrenreich and Deirdre English, *For Her Own Good: Two Centuries of Advice to Women;* e-book (New York, 2005), http://www.feministes-radicales.org/wp-content/uploads/2014/12/Ehrenreich-Barbara-English-Deirdre-For-Her-Own-Good_-Two-Centuries-of-the-Experts-Advice-to-Women-.pdf, 270.

17. Ibid., 271.

18. Amy Cosper, "The Inherent Rebellion of Entrepreneurship," *Entrepreneur,* September 22, 2015, http://www.entrepreneur.com/article/250075.

19. Steve Fraser, *The Age of Acquiescence: The Life and Death of American Resistance to Corporate Power* (New York, 2015), 216.

20. Ibid., 218.

21. Ibid., 255.

22. Karl Marx, *The Eighteenth Brumaire of Louis Bonaparte* (1852); https://www.marxists.org/archive/marx/works/1852/18th-brumaire/ch01.htm.

23. Zygmunt Bauman, *The Individualized Society* (Cambridge, 2001), 18.

24. Ibid., 18–19.

25. The quote is taken from Zygmunt Bauman, *Liquid Modernity* (Oxford, 2000), 65.

26. Ulrich Beck, *Risk Society: Towards a New Modernity* (London, 1992), 137.

27. Ibid., 136.

28. Ibid., 137.

29. Brown, *Undoing the Demos*, 178.

30. Tony Judt, *Ill Fares the Land*, 198.

31. Brown, 222–23.

32. David Boaz, "Key Concepts of Libertarianism," http://www.cato.org/publications/commentary/key-concepts-libertarianism.

33. Dipesh Chakrabarty, "The Climate of History: Four Theses," *Critical Inquiry* 35 (Winter 2009).

34. The term is scattered throughout Jeanson's late writings and interviews. See, for example, Francis Jeanson and Christiane Philip, *Entre-deux* (Bordeaux, 2000); and Francis Jeanson, "Pour une dialectisation du local et du mondial," *Le Passant ordinaire*, September–October 2001.

Chapter 6

1. See my writings on the two volumes of Sartre's *Critique: Jean-Paul Sartre—Philosophy in the World* (London, 1980), 243–86; *Sartre's Second Critique* (Chicago, 1987).

2. This is stressed by the theorist of individualization, Ulrich Beck. See Ulrich Beck and Elisabeth Beck-Gernsheim, *Individualization: Institutionalized Individualism and its Social and Political Consequences* (London, 2002).

3. D. D. Guttenplan, "Why a Left-Wing Socialist Is Poised to Become the Leader of Britain's Labour Party," *The Nation*, Sept 14/21 (2015), 22.

4. Pope Francis, encyclical "Laudato Si" (On Care for Our Common Home) (Rome, 2015), https://w2.vatican.va/content/dam/francesco/pdf/encyclicals/documents/papa-francesco_20150524_enciclica-laudato-si_en.pdf, 194.

5. See http://www.thedailybeast.com/articles/2014/11/07/we-ve-been-on-the -wrong-track-since-1972.html; http://www.gallup.com/poll/1669/general -mood-country.aspx.

6. See Ronald Aronson, *After Marxism* (New York, 1994).

7. Erica Sherover-Marcuse, *Emancipation and Consciousness: Dogmatic and Dialectical Perspectives in the Early Marx* (Oxford, 1986), chapter 1; see the discussion in *After Marxism*, 101–4.

8. Herbert Marcuse, for example, pointed in *Soviet Marxism* (1955) to that fateful moment in the history of Marxism contained in the advent of Leninism, based on Lenin's determination to force the situation, his theoretical separation of a revolutionary vanguard from the mass of the "economist" working class, and the subsequent failure of the German revolution, forecast the future agonies of the Bolshevik Revolution. See *Soviet Marxism* (New York, 1955). See also Ronald Aronson, "The Impermanent Revolution," *The Nation*, February 24, 2005.

9. Sheri Berman, *The Primacy of Politics: Social Democracy and the Making of Europe's Twentieth Century* (Cambridge, 2006).

10. Jean-Paul Sartre, *Critique of Dialectical Reason, II* (London, 2006); Aronson, *Sartre's Second Critique*, 42.

11. Sartre, *Critique of Dialectical Reason*, 351–60.

12. Rebecca Solnit, *Paradise Built in Hell: The Extraordinary Communities That Arise in Disaster* (New York, 2009).

13. Solnit, 305–6.

14. This is influenced by the thinking of Ernst Bloch, but with the decisive difference that Bloch failed to distinguish between intimate personal hopes and social hope.

15. The urban gardening project in Detroit was repeated in 2016, at the same location but with a new group of students. The very small project budget ruled out a trip to the zoo.

16. At the end of the film the miners, defeated in their strike, surprise the gays and lesbians—who by now are themselves fairly depoliticized and concerned only with celebrating their identity—as they join their march, connecting the dots anew. The movie, however, ignores one of the dots to be connected by not mentioning that Mark Ashton, the main organizer of the gays and lesbians, was a member of the Young Communist League.

Postscript

1. Bob Master, "Bernie Sanders, Labor Ideology, and the Future of US Politics," *Truthout*, June 19, 2016, http://www.truth-out.org/news/item /36484-bernie-sanders-labor-ideology-and-the-future-of-us-politics.

2. Obama, 356.

3. Thomas Frank, "Millions of Ordinary Americans Support Donald Trump: Here's Why," https://www.theguardian.com/commentisfree/2016/mar /07/donald-trump-why-americans-support.

4. See Arlie Russell Hochschild, *Strangers in Their Own Land: Anger and Mourning on the American Right* (New York, 2016); and Alexander Zaitchik, *The Gilded Rage: A Wild Ride through Donald Trump's America* (New York, 2016).

5. Rick Perlstein, "Donald Trump and the 'F-Word,'" *Washington Spectator*, September 30, 2015, http://washingtonspectator.org/donald-trump -and-the-f-word/.

6. Brian Beutler, "Can Donald Trump Lead a Political Movement?" *New Republic*, April 12, 2016, https://newrepublic.com/article/132581/can -donald-trump-lead-political-movement.

7. Matthew C. MacWilliams, "How Authoritarianism Took Over the GOP and Allowed for the Emergence of Emperor Trump," *AlterNet*, March 4, 2016, http://www.alternet.org/election-2016/how-authoritarianism-took -over-gop-and-allowed-emergence-emperor-trump.

8. Natalie Jackson, Ariel Edwards-Levy, and Janie Velencia, "Trump Supporters Are More Likely Than Other Republicans to Dislike Minorities," *Huffington Post*, May 17, 2016, http://www.huffingtonpost.com/entry /trump-voters-versus-republicans_us_573b0ec0e4b060aa781b32ce.

Index